WITHDRAWN

Historical Association Studies

Class, Party and the
Political System in Britain
1867–1914

Historical Association Studies

General Editors: M. E. Chamberlain and James Shields

China in the Twentieth Century
Paul Bailey

The Agricultural Revolution
J. V. Beckett

Class, Party and the Political System in
Britain 1867−1914
John Belchem

The Ancien Régime
Peter Campbell

Decolonization
The Fall of the European Empires
M. E. Chamberlain

Gandhi
Anthony Copley

The Counter-Reformation
N. S. Davidson

British Radicalism and the French
Revolution 1789−1815
H. T. Dickinson

From Luddism to the First Reform Bill
Reform in England 1810−1832
J. R. Dinwiddy

Radicalism in the English Revolution
1640−1660
F. D. Dow

Revolution and Counter-Revolution in
France 1815−1852
William Fortescue

The New Monarchy
England, 1471−1534
Anthony Goodman

The French Reformation
Mark Greengrass

Politics in the Reign of Charles II
K. H. D. Haley

Occupied France
Collaboration and Resistance 1940−1944
H. R. Kedward

Secrecy in Britain
Clive Ponting

Women in an
Industrializing Society:
England 1750−1880
Jane Rendall

Appeasement
Keith Robbins

Franklin D. Roosevelt
Michael Simpson

Britain's Decline
Problems and Perspectives
Alan Sked

The Cold War 1945−1965
Joseph Smith

Bismarck
Bruce Waller

The Russian Revolution 1917−1921
Beryl Williams

The Historical Association, founded in 1906, brings together people who share an interest in, and love for, the past. It aims to further the study and teaching of history at all levels: teacher and student, amateur and professional. This is one of over 100 publications available at preferential rates to members. Membership also includes journals at generous discounts and gives access to courses, conferences, tours and regional and local activities. Full details are available from The Secretary, The Historical Association, 59a Kennington Park Road, London SE11 4JH, telephone: 071-735 3901.

Class, Party and the Political System in Britain 1867–1914

John Belchem

Basil Blackwell

First published 1990
First published in USA 1991

Basil Blackwell Ltd
108 Cowley Road, Oxford, OX4 1JF, UK

Basil Blackwell, Inc.
3 Cambridge Center
Cambridge, Massachusetts 02142, USA

British Library Cataloguing in Publication Data
A CIP catalogue record for this book is available from the British Library.

Library of Congress Cataloging in Publication Data

Belchem, John,
    Class, party, and the political system in Britain, 1867–1914/ John Belchem.
    p.   cm. – (Historical Association studies)
    Includes bibliographical references (p.   ).
    ISBN 0–631–15876–6
    1. Great Britain – Politics and government – 1837–1901. 2. Great Britain – Politics and government – 1901–1936. 3. Political parties – Great Britain – History. 4. Social classes – Great Britain – History.
    I. Title. II. Series.
    DA560.B39   1990
    320.941′09′034–dc20   90–278
                                                                    CIP

Typeset in 11 on 13 pt Ehrhardt by Setrite Typesetters Ltd, Hong Kong
Printed in Great Britain by Billing & Sons Ltd, Worcester

Contents

Preface

This short study is designed to introduce students to some of the more complex and controversial issues in recent British political history. By no means a comprehensive political narrative, it extends beyond the narrow focus of the 'high politics' school to assesses the impact of 'class' and the role of 'party' — terms which are examined in the opening chapters — in local, national and Westminster politics. Within these various interlocking arenas, the patterns and codes of political behaviour changed decisively in the period between the Second Reform Act and the First World War. The nature of the changes, however, is hotly debated. Historians are widely at odds in their interpretations of electoral sociology and party performance between 1867 and 1914. This slim introductory volume seeks to elucidate the points of dispute, to encourage students to read more deeply into the controversy. Here attention is drawn to the References and Guide to Further Reading at the end of the study.

John Belchem

1

'Class Politics'

Social class, political scientists maintain, has been the principal line of political demarcation in post-war Britain, the ascendant variable in voting behaviour and party allegiance: 'Class is the basis of British party politics; all else is embellishment and detail' (P. G. J. Pulzer, cited in Wald, 1983, p. 19). Despite recent change in the size and nature of classes, this 'class equals party' model still applies. The working class is declining in size and influence, but as psephological surveys show, class remains a divisive factor in voting behaviour (Waller, 1987). While political scientists speculate on its future, historians have sought to locate the origins of this persistent 'class politics' in late-Victorian Britain.

The language of class entered political discourse in the early nineteenth century, a dynamic replacement for the outdated vocabulary of estates, degrees, orders and ranks. Less rigid than these old social metaphors, the new language was ambiguous in origins and inflexion. Having developed within different models, class meant different things to different people. As articulated by the middle class, it gave expression to social status and pride, a self-conscious social interposition between persons of rank and the common people. For the working class, it was an inevitable fact of life, an identity determined by economic relationships and the labour market. These different constructions — the one social, the other economic — were soon to undermine the united stand of the industrious people, the 'useful and productive classes', against the privileged idle aristocracy. Increasingly at odds with the middle class, the working class developed its own inverted status and pride. All but manual labourers were stigmatized as useless and unproductive once the dignity of labour was subsumed in the language of class. No less proud, non-manual middle-class workers, or 'busy bees', chose to widen the gap between the 'two nations' by insisting on identifying themselves in non-economic, hierarchical terms of relative social position and status. For a brief while, these differences were held in check by the social equipoise of mid-Victorian prosperity, when the language of 'interests' enjoyed a new and temporary vogue. As the economy entered its climacteric in late-Victorian Britain, class returned to dominate social and political discourse. Thereafter, class, status and party, three competing systems of social organization, began to converge, producing the new 'class politics'.

The Victorian language of class was riddled with ambiguity and slippage. Perhaps this accounts for some of the bewildering confusion among historians, social scientists and other commentators on class. In this applied form, the most common (and incorrect) definition of class is still in terms of size and source of income. This was the procedure followed by Ricardo and the classical political economists, proponents of a three-class model of aristocracy, middle class and working class based respectively on rent, profit and wages. Marx was a devastating critic of this crude economism, which ignored the composite nature of income and its myriad forms. To classify by income would lead to an endless and meaningless proliferation of social groups, distinguished by secondary characteristics relating to distribution and consumption. Class, he insisted, was determined by power and property within the productive process, by the relationship to the means of production. Historians, however, are seldom so rigorous. They use class much more loosely as a convenient term for social stratification, a means of classifying groups according to objective measurable criteria: income, housing, diet, education, etc. To deny the terminology of class to these 'social strata' would be unduly pedantic and linguistically inelegant. However, terms should not be confused. Class is by no means restricted to a single stratum. Thus, it is misleading and unnecessary to adopt the plural form, the working classes, simply to acknowledge strata of workers differentiated by income, occupation, region or some other *internal* variable.

The 'class politics' of late-Victorian Britain cannot be understood in the static terms of social stratification. What interests the historian is the complex historical process by which voters, having become conscious of their economic situation, came to recognize a common interest with those similarly placed and a common hostility to those with opposing economic interests. This process of class formation seems to have begun sometime after the Second Reform Act of 1867, as interest, community and religion, the dominant values of the old status or cultural politics, lost their salience (Clarke, 1972). Starting with the Tories, parties fostered a new class awareness, relying for the most part on crude appeals to material interests and status anxieties. In its various partisan forms, populist rhetoric duly acquired a distinctive class inflexion. Unsophisticated but effective, class mobilization at the polls was achieved without any significant advance in ideological expression or elaboration, in the absence of the idealist criteria upon which social scientists and marxist historians insist (Neale, 1981, ch. 1).

The Tories succeeded in attracting the various strata of the propertied middle class, irrespective of the level or source of income. Here the sectional interests of the different fractions of capital — industrial, commercial, financial, rentier, landed, etc. — were of less significance than the security of defensive solidarity against radical finance, socialism and working-class spoliation. The party of property, the Conservatives were increasingly to define themselves against the mythical class enemy, the crude stereotype of a unionized, militant and greedy working class. In this respect, they were keen to hasten the Liberals' downfall, to maximize their electoral strength in straight confrontation with 'working-class' Labour. The party of the 'constitutional classes', the Conservatives offered status and prestige to small property owners, non-manual workers and other marginal lower-middle-class groups, all anxious to distance themselves from the working class below. Here the party benefited substantially from the dramatic increase in the number of clerks, from 95,000 in 1850 to 843,000 in 1914. Unable to secure professional status, institutional protection or salaries higher than the wages of the skilled working class, clerks chose to affirm their gentility through censorious rejection of manual employment, erecting a new caste-like division between those who worked with their hands and those who worked with their brains. Isolated in 'villa Toryism', they segregated themselves from the culture of collective mutuality, street-life and pub-centred leisure enjoyed by well-paid skilled workers and manual labourers alike.

The Liberals, by contrast, favoured a more ideological approach, offering security to the middle class through a programme of social reform which would eradicate class antagonism and pre-empt socialism. By taxing the unearned wealth of parasitic landowners and idle rentiers, reform was to be financed without impeding capitalist enterprise (Emy, 1973). The project was new, but the premiss was outdated. Radical rhetoric continued to posit a fundamental divide between the industrious and the idle, ignoring the increasing unity of propertied interests in late-Victorian and Edwardian Britain. Liberal social radicalism, indeed, frightened the middle-class electorate into defensive Conservative alignment, ironically reinforcing the unwelcome new process of socio-political polarization. Liberals were soon forced to amend their ways, to canvass working-class support to counter both the middle-class drift into Conservatism and the emergence of independent Labour. How well they succeeded as the party of the working class is a matter of considerable controversy in which some historians, much impressed by Edwardian new Liberalism and its strength in industrial Lancashire, question the purpose and prospects not of the Liberals but of Labour (Clarke, 1971). Predicated on 'class politics', this revisionist interpretation, now the new historical orthodoxy (Pugh, 1982), actually minimizes the impact of class. Historians no longer seek to explain the 'strange death' of Liberal England (Dangerfield, 1936), but they should not ignore the stresses and strains of Edwardian class relations. In line with recent studies (Laybourn, 1988, ch. 2), my short survey highlights the class contradictions of progressive Liberalism and the class-based strength of the Labour challenge.

Addressed to the working class through a 'progressive alliance' with Labour, new Liberalism looked to the state to transcend class divisions and promote social harmony. But in ascribing moral and political authority to the state — anathema to unreconstructed *laissez-faire* Liberals — progressive social radicals failed to take account of working-class attitudes and needs. Suspicion of the state ran deep in working-class culture. Hence, Labour's own 'statist' demands were restricted to basic economic fundamentals concerning the right to work, minimum wages and an eight-hour day. Ironically, progressive Liberals refused to intervene on these terms, rejecting Labour's demands as 'sectional', beneath the dignity and higher social purpose of the radical collectivist state. By persisting in this attitude during the pre-war industrial disputes, the new Liberals ruptured what remained of the progressive alliance. Spurned by the interventionist politics of harmony, workers became all the more conscious of their class position (Powell, 1986).

Rising real wages and increased leisure time, the preconditions for the late-Victorian expansion of commercial mass culture, enabled the labour movement to shed its former exclusiveness, to recruit and organize among an increasingly homogeneous working class. As the proportion of the occupied population engaged in agriculture was halved from 15 per cent in 1871 to 7.5 per cent in 1901, rural immigrants entered the most rapidly expanding sectors of the domestic economy, transport and mining, a major shift from worse to better-paid jobs, from less to more regular employment. Regional, skill and gender differentials persisted but the working class acquired a more uniform and modern appearance in the self-enclosed late-Victorian world of flat caps, classic slums and Saturday half-holidays. There was some upward mobility into the lower middle class, but many working-class families, particularly at the top end of the scale, did not regard white-collar employment as an attractive escape from manual labour, a desirable aim for their children. Puny and parasitic, clerks were viewed with derision by skilled workers proud of their transmissible craft and workplace skills. A cultural gulf between two different ways of life, the social separation of skilled workers and clerks reinforced the cultural and political identity of the working class, as the aristocracy of labour, repulsed by lower-middle-class pretensions, turned back to align themselves with their semi-skilled and unskilled manual colleagues (Belchem, 1990, chs 16−20; Hobsbawm, 1984, chs 10−11).

Class identity was reinforced by networks of collective mutuality, self-help agencies which enabled the working class to reduce their insecurity, to 'de-commodify' their labour by means of mutualism, economism and statism. Strategy differed according to local circumstance, the particular alignment of skill, gender and neighbourhood capacities (Savage, 1987, chs 1−2). But there was a clear national trend, a move towards a 'Labour alliance' to provide the funds and framework for independent working-class representation. Having been denied due recognition or proper legal protection, working-class organizations abandoned their traditional Liberal allegiance, rejecting their subordinate status within Lib-Labism to promote their own Labour party. Above all, they looked to Labour to protect the autonomy and traditions of collective voluntarism. Welfare was to be provided not by the servile state but within the democratic conviviality of popular associational culture (Yeo, 1986, pp. 339−44). By no means ideological, support for Labour was a matter of institutional loyalty and defensive class pride, a class consciousness which failed to penetrate to the unorganized casual poor (Hinton, 1982, pp. 25−30).

A two-way process, class politics emerged in late-Victorian Britain as socio-economic factors gained clarity and definition through interaction with the organizational, linguistic and other codes of political behaviour. Shaped by these political structures and traditions, class formation cannot be reduced to crude reductionist analysis. Hence the next chapter examines the crucial features of the political system after 1867.

2

Party and the Political System

Having lost the stigma of factious self-interest, 'party' came to dominate politics after the Second Reform Act, shaping and informing political activity at all levels — at Westminster, in the constituencies and among the electorate. The new party discipline at Westminster, the consequence of procedural change as cabinet extended its authority, terminated the golden age of parliamentary government when ministries — coalitions of shifting groups — were made and unmade by Commons' votes of confidence. Once the main initiators of legislation, private members were whipped to support official party programmes as cabinet assumed legislative as well as executive predominance. The new party discipline extended to the constituencies, though stopping short of the older boroughs and counties: here the politics of deference was to persist long after 1867, operating through nomination, influence and other time-honoured mechanisms (Hanham, 1978, chs 1—3). In the much-enlarged urban constituencies, full-time agents brought professional expertise to party organization. No less important were the new breed of voluntary activists, 'faddists' who abandoned single-issue pressure-group politics in favour of 'entryism', trusting to gain a foothold in the party policy-making process (Hamer, 1977, ch. 4). As it was, party programmes were seldom clearly defined, often no more than a general appeal from the party leader. Even so, voters were invited to choose between parties rather than candidates. Uncontested elections became much less common, while split-voting and non-partisan plumping declined into psephological insignificance as the electorate — enlarged by 88 per cent in 1867 — rapidly adapted to the new party-orientation (Cox, 1987, chs 6, 9–10). Thus, party linked the actions of the rulers with the wishes of the ruled. Previously dependent on parliamentary manoeuvering, coalition-building and votes of confidence, government was legitimized thereafter by popular mandate, by the support the party could command at general election (Bogdanor, 1981, pp. 4–7).

Party politics, now something to be proud of, became the absorbing national passion in the age of Gladstone and Disraeli, popular heroes celebrated on countless plaques, horse brasses, salt cellars, mugs and tiles (Hanham, 1966). Pubs, friendly societies and other collective associations proclaimed their partisan allegiance as society polarized along party lines, a national political culture which embraced all: as Gilbert and Sullivan said in *Iolanthe* (1882),

> . . . every boy and every gal
> That's born into the world alive
> Is either a little Liberal
> Or else a little Conservative!

Party politics spread among the masses, but the electoral process fell far short of a democratic one-man one-vote system. Introduced as a 'leap in the dark' in 1867, household suffrage was extended from the boroughs to the counties by the Third Reform Act (1884), enlarging the electorate by a further 76 per cent. But this was still far from universal manhood suffrage. Until 1918 only about 60 per cent of adult males were entitled to vote, qualifying for one of seven franchises — property, freemen, university, occupation, household, service and lodger. Some were explicitly debarred — lunatics, criminals, aliens, paupers, peers and certain officials concerned with the conduct of elections. Others were indirectly excluded because their accommodation failed to conform to any of the franchise requirements — bachelors living with parents, domestic servants

8

resident with their employers, soldiers living in barracks and the majority of seamen. But most of those denied the vote were kept off the register simply by the complexities of residence and registration requirements, stipulations which served to exclude no less than three million adult males from the general elections of 1910. Strict successive occupation clauses disqualified householders who moved other than within the constituency, while lodgers — who had to apply personally to be put on the register every year — were restricted to a change of room in the one house. Apathy undoubtedly accounted for some non-registration, but the legal sophistry and party chicanery of the registration courts denied many their rights: the average period for provisional registration was calculated as two years one month (Blewett, 1965, p. 35). Here the new Labour party was at a distinct disadvantage, able to afford only 17 full-time agents in 1912 to attend to the complexities of registration procedure (McKibbin, 1974, p. 33).

Labour's poor performance at the polls before 1918 has been attributed to this artificial restriction, 'a franchise and registration system that excluded the greater part of its likely support' (Matthew, McKibbin and Kay, 1976, p. 737). However, most non-voters were not a political class apart. Debarred by technicalities, they would appear on the register from time to time, according to their circumstances and the efforts made by party agents. As for those who were permanently excluded, some 12 per cent of adult males, they were unlikely to benefit Labour: hence the absence of sustained pressure for franchise reform. Outside the ranks of organized labour, the urban casual poor were susceptible to Tory blandishments, vulnerable to charity, patronage and beer, traditional electoral devices of the corrupt old regime. Among poor Irish immigrant communities, a higher level of enfranchisement in Edwardian Britain would have helped the Liberals, not Labour (Pugh, 1982, pp. 141–4).

The 'franchise factor', then, did not entirely operate to Labour's disadvantage, but the electoral system incorporated 'a systematic bias against the working class, not merely a random unfairness to individuals' (Clarke, 1977, p. 582). To a limited extent, age was a countervailing influence by the discrimination in favour of householders as against lodgers. At an early stage in a career structure which required mobility and delayed marriage, some 350,000 or so single middle-class men, mainly lodgers, were without the vote (Tanner, 1983). But other factors reinforced the essential class bias of the system. While the working class and the young were held back by registration, the middle and upper classes exercised the added electoral force of the plural vote, where property qualifications were held in different constituencies. Jealously defended by the Conservatives, this privilege was enjoyed by just over half a million in 1911, about 7 per cent of the electorate. Although concentrated for the most part in commercial and suburban constituencies, the plural vote proved less partisan than assumed: in the elections of 1910, it split somewhere between 6:4 and 7:3 in Conservative favour (Blewett, 1972, p. 363).

Gladstone's failure to abolish the plural vote typified the confused compromise of the electoral reforms of the 1880s, a package of ten bills which comprised the Third Reform Act (Chadwick, 1976). Redistribution was the most significant and contentious issue, the quid pro quo for franchise reform which Salisbury and the Lords would otherwise have blocked. 'Mr Gladstone', the radical Dilke bemoaned, 'was a great conservative on redistribution – the strongest I ever met' (quoted in Bogdanor, 1981, p. 112). Salisbury proved far more radical, appropriating the old Chartist demand for equal electoral districts. In line with earlier exercises in redistribution, he hoped to protect traditional Tory interests, to insulate agricultural representation from urban influences. But as well as the counties, Salisbury wished to divide towns and cities into single-member constituencies, similarly demarcated by 'the pursuits of the population'. Without such redistribution, suburban Conservatives could not compete successfully in major urban centres. Whigs and Radicals were able to run in harness in multi-member constituencies. The limited vote, by which no elector could vote for more than two candidates, failed to protect minority (Tory) interests in three-member city seats. Although introduced as a safeguard in 1867, this 'minority clause' enabled the new Liberal caucus to exploit its canvassing prowess: in Birmingham, for example, the Liberals won all three seats in 1868. As finally agreed by private inter-party conclave, the Redistribution Act (1885) was a compromise between the mathematical formula favoured by Salisbury and the historical principles defended by Gladstone. Small boroughs under 15,000 were disenfranchised; the limited vote was abolished; the ratio of one seat to every 52,000 inhabitants was taken as the average, but 27 two-member constituencies were retained along with one-member seats for established boroughs over 15,000. The worst anomalies were removed: the ratio between the smallest and largest electorates, previously 1:250, was reduced to 1:8. But Gladstone's influence ensured that sparsely populated rural areas received favourable treatment: having benefited most from franchise reform, the Celtic fringe fared best in redistribution, an advantage drastically inflated by continuing demographic decline. By 1915 the ratio between electorates had widened to 1:36 as Kilkenny dropped to 1,702 while suburban Romford mushroomed to 60,878 (Blewett, 1972, pp. 364–5; Kinnear, 1981, p. 70).

Irish over-representation apart, distribution of seats on the principle of representation of numbers, no longer of communities, worked in Conservative favour. Segregated within urban geo-politics, separate suburban seats revealed the strength of 'villa Toryism', a force which Salisbury was the first to perceive. By breaking the mould of political ecology, redistribution was the decisive factor in the late-Victorian transformation of Conservativism: 'Where Conservative supporters had formerly been swamped in huge constituencies, they were now high and dry on islands of their own' (Cornford, 1963, p. 58). The effect in London was particularly dramatic: of the 22 seats available under the old boundaries, Conservatives had secured only 3 in 1868, 10 in 1874 and 8 in 1880; of the 59 seats created by redistribution, they were to gain 35 in 1885, 47 in 1886, 36 in 1892 and 51 in both 1895 and 1900. There was breakthrough too in previously radical provincial cities: in Leeds, Conservatives were to secure two of the five seats, in Sheffield three of the five. By 1900, indeed, the party's principal electoral strength

11

lay in English urban constituencies, where 177 seats were won, overtaking the traditional English county strongholds which supplied 162 seats. In marked contrast to this impressive and enduring urban advance, Liberal revival in the counties proved disappointingly short-lived, a temporary swing at a time of rapid, wide-ranging change. Until others adjusted, Liberals fared best from the introduction of household-suffrage and single-member constituencies, the advent of elected county and parish councils, the democratization of Poor Law authorities and the arrival of popular constituency organizations (Howarth, 1969).

Redistribution allowed suburban Conservatism to flourish, but wider factors accounted for the party's electoral success. Conservative support was spread across the country, a considerable advantage in a single-member plurality system of election by bare majority. This first-past-the-post system was strongly endorsed by Gladstone and Salisbury in reaching the settlement of 1884–5. The best guarantee of party unity and discipline, single-member plurality denied dissidents an independent electoral base out in the constituencies where party machines were in full control. Rebels had either to toe the line or leave and join the other party, a stark alternative which confronted Liberal Unionists and Unionist Free Traders alike. Although frequently mooted, a centre party was not an option. Various alignments were suggested – a party of Radicals led by Chamberlain and Lord Randolph Churchill; a 'moderate constitutional' party led by Hartington and supported by Liberal Unionists and moderate Conservatives; an alliance of Unionist Free Traders and Liberal Imperialists under Rosebery; a union of *laissez-faire* Liberals hostile to Lloyd George's 1909 budget with Unionist Free Traders – but none of these proposals extended much further than dinner-table gossip. New initiatives stood no chance of electoral breakthrough against powerful and solidly entrenched party organizations in the constituencies (Bogdanor, 1981, pp. 111–19). Labour was the one exception, a new party which gained a foothold through the social-geographical concentration of the working-class vote, but even here electoral survival depended upon alliance with the Liberals.

12

Some local activists campaigned for proportional representation, but they received no support from Ramsay MacDonald, theoretician of the 'progressive alliance'. Here, too, party leadership adhered to the existing electoral system to prevent dispute and schism, fearing the election of socialists critical of progressivism (Pugh, 1988, p. 24).

In the absence of proportional representation, the geographical concentrations of anti-Conservative forces led to a great wastage of votes in safe seats. Surprisingly, support for electoral reform — proportional representation, the alternative vote, referendum or some other variant — was restricted to disaffected dissidents, opponents of rigid party discipline. More critical still were the radical right, xenophobic super-patriots whose excoriation of the party system was carried to self-denying demagogic excess. Distrustful of organization, they failed to emerge as an independent force in Edwardian Britain, capable of coordinating their own members and potential supporters among the rapidly expanding lower middle class. Reluctant to break all ties with the Conservative party, they were still bound to parliamentary politics, to the dominant British values of fair play, free speech and toleration (Searle, 1979, pp. 94—6). A similar respect for Parliament, repository of the people's rights, extended across the political spectrum, except perhaps for the pre-war syndicalist fringe. Here the monarchy played a crucial role. Much transformed during Victoria's long reign, the crown was no longer ridiculed and reviled but revered by all as even-handed guarantor of the class neutrality of Parliament and institutions of state (McKibbin, 1984, pp. 310—19). An electoral machine, Labour held firm to parliamentary ways and means, never questioning the rules of the game.

A further factor added to the legitimacy of the system: the gradual, far from complete, elimination of corruption by implementation of the Corrupt and Illegal Practices Act (1883). No longer the preserve of the rich, new-style electioneering depended upon party management and voluntary endeavour, harnessing the resources of those with time and other means to spare. As bribery diminished, the advantages of wealth came

13

into their own, much to Conservative advantage. In 1910, for example, some Tory candidates had over a hundred motor cars at their disposal, transport which facilitated a high turn-out of the plural vote. But the advantage was double-edged: many enjoyed the novelty of a ride in the beribboned and placarded Tory motors, but their anti-Tory vote remained secret, protected by the Ballot Act (1872) (Blewett, 1972, pp. 293−4).

Much time-consuming voluntary work in constituencies was undertaken by women, active participants in politics in all but Parliament itself. By Edwardian times, there was considerable support at Westminster for female suffrage, but no room for manœuvre. Enfranchisement under existing arrangements would restrict the vote to wealthy women, an undue bonus for the Tories. Any comprehensive franchise reform, male and female, would be blocked by the Tories through the Lords' veto, unless accompanied by redistribution, a drastic reduction in Irish seats unacceptable to the Liberal government and its nationalist allies (Pelling, 1979, p. 163). Anger at this impasse prompted the suffragettes, increasingly dominated by Mrs Pankhurst's autocratic daughter Christabel, into unprecedented militancy. The Women's Social and Political Union (WSPU) abandoned links with the Independent Labour Party (ILP) to mount a sensational but socially conservative campaign of middle-class womanhood to coerce the political establishment into conceding 'Votes for Ladies'. Less spectacular but more significant were the radical suffragists, working-class women trained in the trade-union and cooperative movement, who were peaceful campaigners for the vote within a wider frame-work of political and industrial rights. Valuable political experience was gained at local level where they were able to stand for school boards, boards of guardians and other offices (Lidding-ton and Norris, 1978, pp. 134−42).

In local politics there was less discrimination against women, the working class and minority interests. Married women were given the vote on the same terms as men by the Municipal Franchise Act of 1869 which enfranchised all compound rate-payers. Boards were elected by cumulative voting, a system which enabled well-organized minority groups, socialists included, to gain some official representation. Unlike parliamentary elections, no expensive deposit was required for council contests, hence the readiness with which Labour activists, otherwise hard-pressed for funds, encouraged working-class candidates to stand: by 1900, the ILP boasted 106 local councillors, 66 members of school boards and 51 Poor Law guardians (Hinton, 1983, p. 61). With this strong Labour challenge, local politics lost what little remained of their diverse, non-partisan character. Party had already begun to intrude when the Liberal caucus built up grassroots support through ward organization and the capture of councils, school boards and boards of guardians (Fraser, 1979, p. 281). Although localist in rhetoric, the Conservatives were not far behind, using regular council elections to test the efficiency of constituency organization — in 1894, Salisbury issued instructions to make the LCC elections 'a Party fight' (Young, 1975, p. 32). But it was not simply a matter of tactics, a means of 'nursing' constituencies between elections. Policy was very much involved as Conservatives and Liberals were at fundamental odds over the method and amount of local taxation, the crucial issue of 'tenurial politics' separating the parties. (Offer, 1981, chs 15–18.) When confronted by Labour, however, they were to bury these differences in 'anti-socialist' alliance. In local politics, 'progressivism' failed to restrain the Labour advance.

From ward to constituency, politics acquired a national uniformity, but regionalism was not completely eradicated. Party politics developed within an historical geographical pattern. Liberal governments could not normally be formed without a significant presence of Scottish and Welsh Liberal MPs at Westminster, while Conservative ministries normally ruled Britain without majorities in Scotland or Wales (Robbins, 1988, p. 113). The general elections of 1910, the last before the First World War, were merely to accentuate the well-established geo-political division between north and south: 'What was new was that never before had the anti-Unionists done so well in the North, Scotland and Wales, while doing so badly in the South; never before had the Unionists done so well in the South, while doing so badly elsewhere' (Blewett, 1972, p. 381). In some regions, personal influence was the dominant force, as in the West Midlands where Joseph Chamberlain's 'duchy', previously restricted to Birmingham, spread across the Black Country with his advocacy of tariff reform (Pelling, 1967, pp. 201−3). Fuelled by the rabid evangelicalism of the local Anglicans, Lancashire Toryism attracted a large working-class vote. In this heavily industrialized region, religious sectarianism polarized the politics of indigenous workers and immigrant Irish, a pattern accentuated in the Merseyside casual-labour market. Elsewhere, religious affiliation was a less potent force. Conflict between Anglicanism and Dissent, once the very stuff of politics, was of declining relevance, no longer the prime determinant of party allegiance − the Liberals, however, continued to poll well where Nonconformism remained strong, as in the East Midlands (Pelling, 1967, pp. 227−8). A complex process, this 'de-alignment' of politics and religion was accentuated by educational change, by a new mode of socialization based on state-supported, non-sectarian Board schools: 'The old partisan alignment, which had depended upon the transmission of distinctive religiopolitical outlooks in the denominational schools, gave way to a new alignment when the products of the new socialization practices first entered the electorate in large numbers' (Wald, 1983, p. 251).

Religion and regionalism were reduced to the residual as class emerged as the decisive variable. Class politics evolved in the new constituencies of the 1880s, artificial entities which were neither communities in themselves nor administrative units. Here is the challenge for electoral sociologists, researchers who require detailed social data for meaningful political units. Census material was reported from counties, boroughs, Poor Law unions, urban sanitary districts, parishes, etc., a confusing welter of areas which frequently subsumed and often ignored altogether the boundaries of parliamentary constituencies (Wald, 1983, p. 76). Thus, the primacy of class in late-Victorian and Edwardian politics − the dark age between the demise of pollbooks and the appearance of opinion

16

polls — cannot be demonstrated by simple statistics, by direct comparison of electoral and census data. Local studies, however, are indispensable. National patterns of electoral change, the concern of this study, are only aggregates and averages of different local processes.

3

The Conservatives

Once perceived as the party of backwoods agrarianism, the Conservatives were the first to benefit from class politics, attracting the votes and funds of active capital. Alarmed by the prospect of radical Liberalism, the property-holding classes coalesced in defence of security and stability, Conservative values previously upheld by the Palmerstonian centre. This middle-class drift into Conservatism, the most pronounced trend in late Victorian politics, was evident in the aftermath of the Second Reform Act. Liberal and Wesleyan by upbringing, W. H. Smith, a businessman of national celebrity, personified the process. Standing as churchman and Conservative in 1868, he gained election in Westminster, a constituency renowned for its radical past. Smith was a recent convert to the Conservative camp, finally forsaking the family creeds after Palmerston's demise and Gladstone's succession, treading a path which others were soon to follow:

> By 1874 the same change had taken place in individual commercial men all over middle-class London: the City itself, suburban Surrey, Kent and Essex all changed their allegiance, while Middlesex and Westminster each returned two Conservatives by substantial majorities. By 1880 the Liberals had lost control of suburbia altogether. (Hanham, 1978, p. 226)

This accretion of middle-class strength was all the more remarkable in the distinct absence of encouragement from the party leadership. Disraeli's opportunism never strayed beyond the boundaries of traditional Tory interests. By taking on parliamentary reform in 1866—7, he gave the Tories control over redistribution, enabling them to strengthen the electoral weight of the counties while leaving the Liberals to grapple with mass electorates in urban seats. Surprise Tory victories in the boroughs did not alter this traditional frame of mind: under Disraeli's leadership, the Conservatives remained overwhelmingly rural and aristocratic in ethos, attitudes and electoral calculation. Disdainful of the new middle-class conservatism, the party was to vex the patience of John Gorst, its first national agent, responsible through two new bodies — Central Office and the National Union of Conservative and Constitutional Associations — for organization and electoral management, chores previously entrusted to solicitors' firms and party whips. An ardent modernizer, Gorst sought to reshape the party by integrating the new middle-class conservatives of the National Union. His missionary zeal among the urban middle class contributed to the party's success in 1874, but victory was gained through a less positive influence, middle-class reaction against the stresses and strains of Gladstonian Liberalism. Disraeli sensed the mood. Refusing to outbid the Liberals in 'incessant and harassing legislation', he offered order and stability at home, patriotism abroad. The old Palmerstonian formula, now restored to Conservative guardianship, met with suburban approval: 'The middle-class', the *Fortnightly Review* observed, 'has swung round to Conservatism ... The sleek citizens, who pour forth daily from thousands and thousands of smug villas round London, Manchester and Liverpool, read their *Standard* and believe that the country will do very well as it is' (quoted in Dunbabin, 1980, p. 261).

Much to middle-class approval, Disraeli's politics ensured continuity and tradition, befitting his subsequent elevation to the Beaconsfield peerage. In the past, however, his rhetoric

19

had suggested something more exciting, new departures in social reform and imperial grandeur. The basis of much subsequent myth, these occasional opposition speeches were mere opportunism, timely exercises to exploit Liberal disunity and disarm critics in his own party. After 1874 there was no agenda of Tory democracy or expansionist imperialism, only the occasional gesture toward 'one-nation' Conservatism. The new labour laws, for example, were a bold initiative, but there was no further attempt to dislodge the Lib-Labism of the labour aristocracy, to convert the organized and enfranchised working class to the cause of Tory reform. In canvassing the support of workers, the 'angels in marble' (McKenzie and Silver, 1968), Tories continued to rely on old-style populism, the crude appeal to patriotism and Protestantism.

After electoral defeat in 1880 and Beaconsfield's subsequent departure, the party was torn between competing parliamentary and electoral strategies. Northcote, an ineffectual leader in the Commons, favoured conciliation and consensus, tactics which would hasten party reconstruction by attracting the Whigs into Conservative alliance. Such supine parliamentarianism was ridiculed and repudiated by the 'Fourth Party', a group of talented politicians — Lord Randolph Churchill, H. D. Wolff, Gorst and others — brought together to uphold Tory 'Church and King' principles against Bradlaugh's atheist-republicanism, but identified thereafter with the new conservatism of the urban constituencies. The first to evoke the myth of Disraelian 'Tory democracy', Churchill, the most talented and ambitious of the group, sought to exploit for his own political ends intra-party tensions between parliamentary leadership and constituency organization. As chairman of the National Union Council, he demanded policies and procedures which recognized the worth of urban conservatives, still slighted and ignored by the parliamentary party:

Unfortunately for Conservatism, its leaders belong solely to one class; they are a clique composed of members of the aristocracy, landowners and adherents whose chief merit is subserviency. The party chiefs live in an atmosphere in which a sense of their own importance and the importance of their class interests and privileges is exaggerated, and which the opinions of the common people can scarcely penetrate. (Quoted in Coleman, 1988, p. 167)

In fear of a Liberal-style caucus, Salisbury decided to buy Churchill off, inviting him to join the party's collective leadership: successful negotiations from which the hapless Northcote was excluded.

SALISBURY AND THE UNIONIST ALLIANCE

Aristocratic and assured, Salisbury's conservatism eschewed both parliamentary centrism and electoral opportunism. Convinced that the Whigs would fall into the Conservative camp sooner or later, he refused to canvass their support, to moderate policy in pursuit of realignment. While Northcote favoured consensus, Salisbury sought to polarize politics, preserving party integrity through uncompromising defence of established interests. Similarly with electoral politics he refused to make concessions, to endorse new policies and procedures simply to promote the urban Tory vote. Having resigned in fearful alarm over the Second Reform Act, he took some reassurance from villa Toryism, but he still distrusted reform. In his Conservative frame of mind, 'Tory democracy' would lead ineluctably to the dispossession of the wealthy, whatever its form or short-term advantage. But redistribution offered a safe alternative: new boundaries, not new policies, were the key to the future.

Redistribution was a triumph for Salisbury. His hard bargaining not only confirmed his undisputed leadership of the party, but also produced a settlement geared to the suburban geo-politics of middle-class conservatism. To derive maximum advantage, the new Conservatives were at last accorded recognition and status within party organization. Power and influence remained out of reach, but middle-class activists were granted sufficient acknowledgement to defuse the tensions

21

exploited by Gorst and Churchill. As part of this conciliation process, constituency associations were reorganized by 'Captain' Middleton, the new Principal Agent and secretary of the National Union. Full-time agents were appointed to tackle the complexities of registration, while local volunteers received a regular supply of posters, pamphlets and helpful advice from Central Office. Lacking political ambitions of his own, Middleton, working in alliance with Akers-Douglas, the new chief whip, was a tireless campaigner for a more professional approach to party organization. Previously ill-disposed towards such matters, Salisbury was disabused of his patrician prejudices by the efficiency of the 'Middleton machine'. Operating from the centre downwards, party organization was the best security against caucus control, the most effective means to educate and restrain the electorate. A new enthusiast, Salisbury looked to organization to ensure the discipline of popular government (Marsh, 1978, ch. 6).

Under Salisbury's leadership, the Tories consolidated their hold on the middle-class vote, turning the new electoral system to party advantage without abandoning traditional interests and objectives. From 1885 to 1910, the Conservative or Unionist vote was consistently high in the 56 wealthiest constituencies, those in which at least one female domestic servant was employed for every four families, the six-election median average registering 58.6 per cent (Pelling, 1967, p. 418). Matters of power and policy apart, the middle class were everywhere in the ascendant, gaining recognition and status not only in constituency associations and national organizations but even on the parliamentary benches — a substantial majority of each new set of Conservative recruits to the Commons after 1885 was drawn from the professional and industrial middle classes (Cornford, 1967). Senior ministerial appointments, however, tended to remain socially exclusive. Here, as in his private life, Salisbury was no less snobbish than Lord Randolph Churchill, avoiding the company of the business plutocracy, the 'Marshall and Snelgrove' element of the government. Even so, there was a marked change in the social composition of the cabinet: between 1880 and 1895, cabinets contained 47 aristocratic and

30 middle-class members; between 1895 and 1905 the numbers were 17 and 21 respectively (Guttsman, 1963, p. 78). Less inhibited than his predecessors, Salisbury indulged in a 'rage of honours', symbolic recognition of the financial and other contributions of the urban plutocracy. Peerages, baronetcies and knighthoods were bestowed in unashamedly partisan manner on Conservative financiers, brewers, distillers, shipping magnates, merchants and industrialists. The most aristocratic of nineteenth-century prime ministers, Salisbury was to unite 'the classes' against 'the masses'.

Salisbury's hold on power depended upon the Unionist alliance, a parliamentary realignment secured without conciliation or concession. The Irish question had already added to middle-class anxieties: feared as a dangerous precedent, Gladstone's land reforms brought property holders together in Conservative defence of their rights. Salisbury's hard-line stance throughout the Home Rule crisis, however, was determined more by parliamentary than by electoral considerations. Above all, he was resolved to thwart Hartington, a Whig who aspired to reconstruct the moderate centre by means of either a 'Palmerstonian' ministry of Liberals reunited in the absence of Gladstone (and his Irish obsession), or through broader cross-bench alliance, a centrist coalition incorporating moderate Conservatives. To isolate the centrists, Salisbury polarized the parties, abandoning the ambivalent tone of recent Tory negotiations with nationalist leaders to advocate hard-line reaction. His famous 'manacles and Manitoba' speech, a calculated affront to Whig traditions of reformism, prescribed 20 years of 'resolute government' for the Irish whose capacity for self-rule was on a par with the Hottentots, and whose economic woes would best be solved by emigration to Manitoba. Intended as a rallying-point for Liberals and moderates, opposition to Home Rule was henceforth identified with Tory reaction, a debilitating stigma which Hartington was unable to eradicate. As for Conservatives, defence of the Union was no longer an issue for coalition discussion, but the very test of party loyalty (Cooke and Vincent, 1974, ch. 3).

After Gladstone's defeat on Home Rule, Salisbury secured

an electoral compact with Liberal Unionists. The arrangement confirmed their separation from the Gladstonian Liberal party, while keeping them apart from Conservative control of government. Thanks to Middleton's influence, Conservative associations were persuaded to support sitting Liberal Unionist MPs at the 1886 general election. But there were no further concessions or favours even though the Conservatives fell short of an overall Commons' majority. Salisbury had no wish to jeopardize his party principles and personal position in parliamentary coalition under Liberal Unionist domination — only 79 of their number were returned in 1886, but they were disproportionately strong in administrative and debating talent. As leader of the Conservatives, the party of resistance, Salisbury took command of government, waiting for Liberal Unionists to fall in line. Hard-line but patient, his conservative politics reaped rich rewards:

> His strongly toned Conservatism, far from hindering an alliance, won greater confidence from Whig and moderate Liberal Unionists than they would have reposed in any Conservative who bid for the middle ground ... When, many years later, fusion occurred, the amalgamated party was to be recognizably Conservative. (Marsh, 1978, p. 137)

For a brief while, Lord Randolph Churchill canvassed support for a more adventurous course, a radical alliance with Chamberlain and Liberal Unionists to outbid the Liberals in modern programme politics. As Chancellor of the Exchequer, he drew up a progressive budget embodying the principles of 'peace, retrenchment and reform', the radical platform which he now wished to appropriate. Having antagonized party traditionalists, he offered his resignation to force the issue, tactics which backfired as Salisbury seized the opportunity to eradicate the radical threat. Caught unprepared, Churchill was unable to regain office and influence, a fall from power which left Chamberlain — and his Birmingham nostrums — without friends in high places. At the Exchequer, Churchill was replaced by Goschen, a senior Liberal Unionist and former minister closely associated with Hartington, whose continuing support for the government was thereby assured. The only Liberal Unionist in the ministry, Goschen, a former banker and City MP, brought financial expertise and ideological appeal to the Unionist alliance, personifying as it were the new financial and commercial conservatism. Having hoped to restructure and strengthen the non-Tory right, he now joined Salisbury's Conservatives to defend property and free enterprise, values not to be jeopardized by radical Liberalism or 'Tory democracy'.

Through his 'executive Conservatism', Salisbury supervised the political fusion of landed, commercial and industrial wealth, offering 'the defence of property, social and political stability, a minimum of government interference, and the bland professionalism of the true politician which bred business confidence' (O'Gorman, 1986, p. 39). By doing so little, Salisbury's party provided a safe haven for propertied opinion, a refuge against mass enfranchisement, the Nonconformist conscience, radical Liberalism and the socialist spectre. In late-Victorian Conservatism, conservation and ordered change, the old Burkeian ideals, were of far less account than the defence of property. As trade unions and collectivism advanced remorselessly, Conservative thinkers, Salisbury included, became obsessed with the socialist threat, turning for security to the liberal and individualist values they had previously opposed.

Conservatives sacrificed none of their traditional interests, but adapted their ideology to embrace the wider security of property, in line with contemporary economic and social change. As agricultural depression persisted, falling rents encouraged landowners to pursue other forms of income, removing what remained of social, cultural and political barriers within the framework of distinctively British 'gentlemanly capitalism' (Cain and Hopkins, 1987, pp. 4–11). The 'demon of gentility' drew northern industrialists, or rather their sons, into this southern-based, public-school, gentry culture of landed and City wealth. Conservatism prospered as the City expanded, injecting considerable impetus into the regional service economy of London and the suburban south-east, the most dynamic area of growth, no longer overshadowed by the (Liberal) industrial provinces (Anderson, 1987; Daunton, 1989; Wiener, 1985). The 'upper section of society', the *Spectator* noted in 1894, 'is becoming dangerously unanimous ... The squires are as single-minded as the peers, and so in the main are the new millionaires, the great merchants, the whole class down to a much lower stratum than is usually believed, of what may be called "solid men"' (quoted in Burgess, 1980, p. 95).

Once incorporated into the party, the 'lords of the suburban villas' served to strengthen, not to challenge, traditional Conservatism. Dutiful and loyal to party leadership and policies, middle-class constituency activists, unlike their 'faddist' Liberal counterparts, concentrated their energies on branch-building, propaganda and speech-making. In the absence of constituency pressure from below, the Conservatives were untroubled by narrow and contentious programme politics. Although clearly middle-class, the party was not burdened with an ideological class manifesto. The party, indeed, could still bid for wider support, continuing to evoke the rhetoric of 'one nation', populist language which proudly transcended class.

POPULAR CONSERVATISM

Popular support was cultivated through a variety of paternalistic strategies, contrasting cultural styles geared to different audiences. In manly and squirely form (a genre favoured by northern industrialists), Tory paternalism championed the working man's right to a glass of beer and his idle pastimes (Joyce, 1982, pp. 189—91). The Tories, guardians of popular culture, were masters of the politics of entertainment and *bonhomie*, offering a range of attractions which Liberals, secularists and socialists, divided over temperance and ascetic considerations, were unable to match. While the middle-class patrons of the non-political Club and Institute Union, soberminded 'rational recreationalists', tried to resist popular pressure for drink and entertainment, promoters of Conservative working-men's clubs allowed their grateful members to enjoy cheap 'bacca, billiards and beer'.

The Primrose League offered different fare: tea and sandwiches partaken in country houses and on vicarage lawns, where genteel paternalism elicited snobbery and deference, good Conservative values. Not a matter for apology, class was a positive virtue in the League, deliberately emphasized by differential ranks and fees, a mock-medieval hierarchy of humble Primrose Buds, Dames, Vavasours, Knights Almoner and Knights Companion. Within this artificial structure, humble Conservatives of the lower classes were able to indulge their fascination with the lives of the high-born and wealthy, dignitaries who graced the lantern-shows, concerts, tea parties, garden parties and other social functions organized by the local 'habitation'. By 1900 there were 2,300 habitations, with over 1.5 million members, by far the largest political organization of the time, particularly strong in rural and suburban areas where clubs and registration societies were thin on the ground. In 1906 the Bolton branch with 6,000 paid members matched the total national paid membership of the Independent Labour Party! (Pugh, 1985b, p. 2). Extensive leisure and benefit facilities attracted the widest possible membership, non-voters as well as voters, the apathetic as well as the political, women as well as men, but party purpose was not forgotten. Each local branch of the Primrose League Cycling Corps helped ensure the remarkable stability of the Conservative vote by tracing removals on the electoral register, contacting isolated voters and conveying messages between committee rooms. Brainchild of Churchill and the 'Fourth Party', the League was initially regarded with some suspicion, but party leaders were quick to appreciate both its propaganda and its electoral value, all the more useful after the 1883 Corrupt and Illegal Practices Act, and its docility on matters of policy. Formed to elicit popular support for the traditional props of Conservatism, the League propounded an uncontentious, vague and popular brand of patriotism, imperialism and monarchy, the Tory 'spirit of the age'. Along with the efforts of the League, popular imperialist

27

propaganda took a variety of forms in late-Victorian Britain, from music-hall songs and juvenile comics to advertising slogans and commercial packaging, with the benefits of Empire depicted on biscuit tins, cigarette packets and other symbols of the retail revolution.

Outside these paternalistic strategies and associational forms, many working-class electors voted Conservative for pragmatic or ideological reasons. Defenders of ancient privileges, Tories attracted the support of workers whose livelihoods depended on continuing restrictive rights and monopolies, hence the Conservatism of London watermen and lightermen, and of metropolitan costermongers who regarded their pitches as 'freeholds'. Other workers — Coventry ribboners, Nottingham lace-makers, Boston fishermen, midland and Sheffield metal workers — looked to the Tories for protection against in-creasing foreign competition (Pelling, 1967). In such trades Conservative allegiance persisted, little diminished by the party's increasingly harsh stance on labour relations. Backed by Halsbury's partisan appointments to the judicial bench, the Conservatives had clearly emerged by the 1890s as the party of opposition to trade-union demands (Coleman, 1988, p. 197). Once identified with anti-trade-unionism, however, the party was less successful in tapping working-class 'economism', a powerful force in towns like Preston where Conservatives 'did not attempt to play down class divisions but merely harnessed them to their own ends ... Toryism made no bones about accepting the reality of class, simply emphasising that working-class interests were served by local employers able to provide employment' (Savage, 1987, p. 143). In the lower reaches of the service sector, obsequious subservience continued to breed instinctual deference, as expressed by a college servant at King's Cambridge: 'Well, sir, for as simple as I am, I've always heard there was never better times than when the Conservatives was in power' (Hammerton and Cannadine, 1981, p. 121). Most 'traditionalists' among the working class tended to vote Conservative, although their acceptance of the political status quo was often accompanied by distrust of those who main-tained it. At this ideological level, working-class Conservatism

28

needs to be studied in what has been called 'a wider context of shared incoherence' (Lee, 1979, p. 96).

TARIFF REFORM

Having adjusted to class politics without sacrificing traditional interests or the popular vote, Conservatives had then to restrain middle-class ideologues and populist demagogues. Activists of the patriotic lobby failed to advance to positions of power and influence, kept at bay by party managers averse to emotive rhetoric and divisive policies. Anti-Catholicism continued in traditional form, ensuring a substantial Tory working-class vote in areas of heavy Irish immigration, but the rabid anti-alienism of the patriotic platform, directed against new arrivals from eastern Europe, was altogether different, an unacceptable form of racism. Within the dominant political culture, there was a taboo on the *open* expression of anti-Semitic views. The patriotic lobby was also linked with the unacceptable face of 'fair trade', sponsoring the murky and corrupt activities of anti-trade-unionists whom Middleton considered 'utterly untrustworthy' (Cunningham, 1986, pp. 287–8). Far more respectable, but no less contentious, were the protectionist proposals which found favour in the National Union, a body otherwise compliant on matters of policy. Through tariff reform and the National Union, Chamberlain was soon to attempt to modernize politics, to replace Conservatism with radical and constructive Unionism.

Chamberlain, a Birmingham screwmaker, retained a troublesome independence after 1886, while Whigs and other Liberal Unionists gradually coalesced with Conservatives into a unified social and political elite. His radical reputation, the title to his 'duchy', precluded any close association with the Conservatives. Hence, his support for the ministry on votes of confidence and over Home Rule was carefully balanced by displays of dissent and contrariness, tactics which secured a number of radical concessions, much to Salisbury's increasing irritation. Brought into government in 1895 in a symbolic strengthening of the

29

Unionist alliance, he briefly eschewed 'sensational legislation' to concentrate on his colonial portfolio. The appeal of imperialism, however, diminished considerably once the Boer War exposed national inefficiency and physical deterioration. Amid the mood of national introspection, as Balfour's government faltered between the need to reduce high wartime taxation and to raise revenue for social reform, Chamberlain stood forward to advocate tariff reform.

Addressed to long-term problems of economic, imperial and military decline, Chamberlain's programme − based on colonial preference − held out the prospect of industrial regeneration and imperial economic unity, while providing funds not only for social reform but also for Dreadnoughts. Much less narrow than earlier 'fair trade' proposals, his scheme endeavoured to fuse industrial and landed interests, but it still exposed fractures in the Unionist alliance. By comparison with the previous policy of the aristocratic 'charmed circle', the emollient inaction of the 'Hotel Cecil' (Cornford, 1967), tariff reform was radical and divisive, championing productive capital at the expense of the City, finance capital and the fixed incomes of fundholders and rentiers. Balfour's middle-of-the-road pronouncements could not conceal these fundamental divisions, making the party appear at the polls to be both hesitant and divided. This uncharacteristic and debilitating image led to humiliating defeat, compounded by the exceptional Liberal unity in defence of free trade − in this respect, the 1906 result pointed to the negative nature of the late-Victorian Conservative hegemony, based on Liberal failure to bring out their vote, to stem abstention, rather than on defection (Blewett, 1972, p. 22).

In ironic response to this defeat, the parliamentary party became more ardent in support of tariff reform. The new fervour was not of Chamberlain's making: he had been forced to withdraw from active politics after a paralytic stroke. It was fear of the alternative which underpinned the new enthusiasm. Confronted by 'new Liberalism', Conservatives upheld tariff reform as the best defence against 'socialist' redistribution, a means of financing necessary social reforms and rearmament without recourse to confiscatory taxation and punitive land duties. As Edwardian politics polarized over finance, the abandonment of free trade seemed a much lesser evil than graduated taxation. Recast in Conservative mould, tariff reform offered reassurance to all property-holders, reunited in defensive solidarity against Liberal finance (Sykes, 1979, p. 6). Although specifically directed against rent and landed tenures, the progressive thrust of Liberal finance provoked considerable anxiety throughout the propertied classes, extending down to the lower middle class. Tariff reform assuaged their fears, keeping the small property-owners loyal to party politics at a time when their continental counterparts turned to extremist organizations. In the absence of a militant *Mittelstand*, the British radical right failed to develop alternative, extra-parliamentary tactics. Backed by large-scale business interests, the Liberty and Property Defence League and the Anti-Socialist Union sought to strengthen Conservative resolve (Crossick, 1977, p. 41).

Diehard resistance was the order of the day when Conservative peers rejected Lloyd George's 'People's Budget' of 1909, in defiance of history and of constitutional precedent. By finding revenue for social reform and the navy without abandoning free trade, the budget undermined the central thrust of tariff-reform argument. Modest in themselves, the land-tax proposals were quite unacceptable to Conservative peers, being linked to land valuation, the necessary preparation for something far worse: radical and comprehensive land reform. Although forced into wild negativism by Lloyd George's rhetorical command of this unplanned constitutional crisis, the Conservatives still managed to recoup some electoral support, obliging the Liberals to go to the country twice in 1910, at the cost of their overall majority. They changed tack before the second election, recognizing that tariff reform, taxes on food, was still a liability among a popular electorate reared on free trade and cheap bread. Balfour's pledge to hold a referendum on the question encouraged a few Lancashire working-class constituencies back into the fold, but the December results confirmed the earlier verdict, leaving the Liberals in power, but dependent on the support of Labour and the Irish nationalists. Tariff reform lost its symbolic importance as Home Rule returned to the top of the political agenda: defence of the Union was once again the essential Conservative cause (Sykes, 1979, p. 258).

BONAR LAW

Deprived of the Lords' veto, Unionists were compelled to adopt other tactics to protect the Union: obstruction, threats and offensive behaviour in the Commons, and mutinous extra-parliamentary activity carried to the very verge of civil war. Having dispensed with Balfour's services, the party chose as his successor Bonar Law, a compromise candidate who soon came to personify the tough and abrasive 'new style'. Born in the far-flung Empire, Law, the son of a Presbyterian minister of Ulster origin in New Brunswick, was neither an Anglican nor a landowner. Having been brought up by his mother's family in Scotland, he had made his own way in the Glasgow iron trade. Blunt and vigorous, he threw restraint to the winds. His atavistic extremism over Ulster served to unify and re-generate the party, while placating the extreme right who might otherwise have abandoned the parliamentary party system al-together. The constitution was strained to the limit as the Conservatives, frustrated by three successive electoral defeats, sought revenge on the Liberals who had not played fair by their secret deals with Labour. But in fanning the extremist mood, Law did not ignore the realities of electoral politics: he supervised a major overhaul of party machinery to strengthen the Conservative vote against the 'progressive alliance'. New personnel were brought in at the top: by 1912, the Conserva-tives had a new chief whip, party chairman, party treasurer, principal agent and press adviser, officers through whom con-stituency opinion could be measured and influenced. In place of conventional preoccupation with registration, constituency organization was directed towards political education and pro-paganda, an all-out drive to convert voters already on the register. Agents from Central Office encouraged these modern attitudes at constituency level, assisted by close contact with Fleet Street and the press — secret intelligence departments were set up in each area, with a press bureau to maintain regular liaison with journalists and editors. To streamline the initiative, competing bodies were coordinated in a new party structure: the National Union was merged with Central Office in 1911; a year later, Conservatives and Liberal Unionists finally fused as the Conservative and Unionist party (Middlemas, 1979, p. 40; Ramsden, 1978, chs 4–5).

Reorganization was one factor in the party's success at the polls in the immediate pre-war years, a time when its leadership seemed intent on self-destruction, challenging the very practice and authority of Parliament. But election results must be judged within the context of mid-term fluctuations of opinion: there is insufficient psephological evidence on the eve of the First World War to suggest that the Conservatives were certain of victory at the next general election. At municipal level, however, they were certainly in the ascendant, boosted by tensions in the 'progressive alliance' and by new anti-Labour pacts with their erstwhile Liberal foes. The most constant factor of pre-war local elections 'was not primarily the Liberal decline (real though it was) nor the rise of Labour (patchy and unimpressive as this often was) but rather the strength of Conservatism' (Cook, 1976, p. 63). At this level, Conservatism fed on the fear of socialist advance, of expensive municipal programmes for the benefit of the idle and work-shy, the poor and unemployed. This was the 'class politics' which the Conservatives were to perfect in inter-war Britain, attracting the middle-class vote by a crude portrayal of the working-class threat.

Alternative forms of Conservatism, however, still attracted support within the party. Hoping to regain the working-class vote lost in 1910, the Unionist Social Reform Committee, the party's think-tank, refused to restrict Conservatism to the negative defence of middle-class interests. Chaired by F. E. Smith, the Committee advocated constructive social reform but without tariff reform, the electoral liability of 'food taxes'.

33

Social policy was to be financed through 'grants-in-aid', a progressive alternative to regressive and unjust local rates. Heirs of the 'one nation' Tory democracy of Disraelian myth, the Committee sought a third alternative to Lloyd George's 'Radical-Socialism' and 'Whig Individualism', a reconciliation of class interests under a higher national and imperial unity (Ridley, 1987). Hence their willingness to conciliate the trade unions, to incorporate working-class associations in the 'politics of industrial society' (Middlemas, 1979). Some of the Committee's proposals were included in the *Campaign guide* prepared for the forthcoming election, but the First World War intervened, enabling the Conservatives to conceal their class character and expand beyond their solid middle-class base simply by command of the rhetoric of patriotism.

4

The Liberals

Inaction, the Conservative formula for success in the new class politics, was not an option for the Liberals, a party founded in progressive sentiment. A gamut of 'out-groups' — religious, occupational, regional and national — kept the party true to its colours, a reforming force to curb the privilege of 'old corruption', the continuing dominance of the landed, Anglican and English establishment (Vincent, 1972, p. 33). Liberals, then, could not afford to offend Nonconformist, Celtic or other susceptibilities: although unlikely to vote Tory, these sectional blocs might well abstain, a potent weapon of protest in a plurality system. Here a more serious threat was posed by the faddists, political enthusiasts whose services were indispensable in turning out the Liberal vote in the large urban constituencies. Having abandoned pressure-group politics for entryism, these incorruptible radicals, or 'anti-everythingarians', looked to the Liberals to prioritize their particular nostrum — temperance, disestablishment, secular education, international peace, repeal of the Contagious Diseases Act, or whatever. Refusing to accept compromise or delay from Liberal government, they were wont to withdraw their labours at the next election, retreating in disillusion until confronted by the harsh reality of Tory victory (Hamer, 1972, ch. 1).

Progressive sentiment and faddist enthusiasm, the distinguishing virtues of the party's formative period, were thus volatile forces, causing considerable fluctuations in the Liberal vote. But behind these ups and downs, the more prescient Liberals discerned a middle-class drift towards Conservatism, a disturbing trend which they were determined to reverse. Acknowledging the need for security, they offered the middle class an imaginative alternative, a programme of social reform which would remove class antagonism and thereby prevent the otherwise inevitable socialist challenge. Pre-emptive in function, collectivism was to be financed without impeding capitalist enterprise, by taxing the unearned wealth of landowners and rentiers. Phrased in the language of class harmony, this new Liberalism was predicated on the old radical division — the sociological foundation of both Chartist and Anti-Corn Law League rhetoric — between the industrious and the idle. Previously relevant, the distinction was increasingly anachronistic in late-Victorian Britain as property interests merged, united in Conservative defence against the exactions of radical-cum-socialist finance. Counter-productive in its appeal to the middle class, new Liberalism was to acquire enhanced importance in the struggle to retain the working-class vote, the party's last best hope. The extent to which the Liberals succeeded in adjusting to working-class politics, in containing independent Labour, will be examined in the study of Liberal—Labour relations in the next chapter. First, it is necessary to trace the origins of progressivism within the context of internal tensions and competing strategies.

GLADSTONE AND THE POLITICS OF MORAL PASSION

Gladstone's radicalism, the product of lengthy intellectual and religious agonizing, was never in doubt after the setback of 1866—7 when Disraeli had briefly seized the initiative. From opposition, Gladstone was able to rally the party, uniting the various blocs, sections and activists in the first of his great 'wars of religious liberalism'. These campaigns relied for their success on his remarkable rhetorical force, his ability to subsume sectional and divisive interests in the politics of moral passion. Eschewing any crude appeal to class, Gladstone invoked a wider frame of reference, a single overarching issue — Irish disestablishment, the evils of Beaconsfieldism, Irish Home Rule — within which individuals, sections and classes could transcend the narrow limits of their own 'selfish' interests. Here ideology coincided with electoral realism. The foe of sinfulness, selfishness and fiscal extravagance, Gladstone campaigned against the abuse of power and privilege, attracting the votes of those who enjoyed neither, subservient small shopkeepers and tradesmen, the 'individualist' voters who still dominated most electoral rolls. Averse to increased taxation, they were uninterested in social reform — dismissed by Gladstone as divisive and expensive — but they relished the opportunity to exact political revenge, to belittle the high and mighty at the polls. In his electoral crusades, Gladstone, the 'people's William', offered the 'psychic satisfaction of ruling to the ruled' (Vincent, 1967, p. 45).

Broadcast by the press, Gladstone's rhetoric flattered and exalted the moral and intellectual capacities of 'the people', duly enlisted in the campaign for political justice. His wars of religious liberalism were to maximize popular participation in politics, the final climax of radical populism before commercial mass culture, with its Tory connections, asserted its primacy. At the polls, Gladstone was the Liberals' greatest asset, but victory was always to be followed by shambles and disarray in office. In the absence of an agreed programme beyond disestablishment of the Irish Church, Gladstone's first ministry muddled through a series of measures to curb monpoly, remove social abuses and promote desirable behaviour, *ad hoc* legislation which antagonized the Whigs while disappointing the Radicals. As a gesture of protest, a significant number of constituency activists withdrew their services, but the party's defeat in 1874 shocked them back into action. From the ruins of the National Education League, one of several disillusioned pressure groups, Joseph Chamberlain constructed the National Liberal Federation (NLF), an ambitious attempt to radicalize party policy and organization. Infuriated by Gladstone's style of party management, Chamberlain sought to introduce 'programme politics', transferring power to the new local party associations. No longer the preserve of time-serving oligarchies, local associations had passed into faddist control, as at Birmingham where the model democratic structure was manipulated and controlled by a powerful Chamberlainite 'caucus'. The NLF was expected to operate in similar fashion, an institutional umbrella to co-ordinate and rank the various reforms demanded by party activists out in the constituencies. Chamberlain, however, was to be frustrated in his ambitions. Having returned from retirement to protest against the Bulgarian atrocities, Gladstone graced the platform at the inaugural NLF conference in 1877, promptly captivating the delegates with his impassioned denunciation of Beaconsfieldism, prestige politics and the wicked Turk. By keeping his grip on radical affections, especially in foreign and imperial affairs, Gladstone was able to thwart caucus control and programme politics.

Virtuous and impassioned, his Midlothian rhetoric served once again to transcend Whig inertia and radical impatience, carrying the Liberals back into power in 1880 on a wave of moral righteousness. Lacking any manifesto other than the negative mandate to undo Beaconsfieldism, the Liberals were soon at odds again over policies and priorities, divisions which deepened as an unfortunate conjuncture of colonial, Irish and domestic problems took Gladstone's attention further away from party management and reform. Divided and discredited, the government was finally defeated over the 1885 budget, but elections were delayed pending the completion of the new registers of the Fourth Reform Act. The new electoral possibilities of the Act, the one positive achievement of the ministry, encouraged the Radicals to bid for power. Chamberlain resigned shortly before the ignominious ministerial collapse, to canvass support for the 'Radical Programme', a comprehensive alternative to official party policy. A platform of planks, this 'Unauthorized Programme', as it was henceforth known, sought to dispense with old issues through devolution and local government reform, enabling the party to progress to 'Free Church, Free Land, Free Schools and Free Labour'. Some aspects of this 'quadrilateral' were advanced or 'constructive', a new type of interventionist radicalism which owed much to Chamberlain's experience of 'municipal socialism' in Birmingham, where public enterprise was responsible for gas, water, sewerage, lighting and slum clearance. Here was the 'ransom' — social reform and limited collectivism funded by graduated taxation, death duties and other financial reforms — which property had to pay to ensure security of tenure. In this respect, the 'Unauthorized Programme', like tariff reform later, was an ambitious exercise in pre-emptive politics, a clarion call to the middle class to prevent class polarization and socialist dispossession. Through constructive social reform, the radical programme would ensure social harmony, keeping the working and middle classes united, the industrious and productive sectors of society whose worth was still denied by parasitic landowners and idle rentiers, 'those who toil not, neither do they spin.'

In demonizing the landlord, Chamberlain and his colleagues struck a familiar radical chord, all the more resonant as household suffrage was extended to the counties. Through compulsory purchase by local authorities, the programme held out the promise of 'three acres and a cow' to the new rural voters. Urban workers were offered less tangible benefits, a programme of reform little in advance of traditional Liberalism, the 'Radicalism of the crotchet-mongers' (Hamer, 1971, p. xxxi). In the absence of an 'urban cow', the programme failed to arouse enthusiasm among the working class. At the Industrial Remuneration Conference in 1885, J. E. Williams, a member of the Social Democratic Federation, ridiculed the initiative: 'The Radical today was the "Artful Dodger" who went up and down the country telling the people to take hold of the landlord thief but to let the greater thief, the capitalist go scotfree' (quoted in Clegg, Fox and Thompson, 1964, p. 53). To the middle-class electorate, however, the programme was too advanced, the thin end of the socialist wedge. Having failed to attract and unite the productive classes, Chamberlain was ill-placed to continue the Radical challenge. An electoral liability, his credentials were compromised further by his aggressive stance on foreign and imperial issues, a maverick approach which antagonized parliamentary colleagues, Radicals reared on the creeds of Cobden and Bright. Lacking an adequate power base, he entered negotiations with Hartington, trusting to secure a position of influence (not least over domestic reform) once the latter assumed the leadership. Contrary to expectations, however, Gladstone chose not to retire, or to allow himself to be ousted. No less than Salisbury, the Grand Old Man was to exploit the high political crisis of 1885–6 to devastating effect. By elevating Home Rule to a moral crusade, he occupied the Radical high ground, establishing a criterion which Chamberlain and the Whigs were unable to meet. A test of Liberal orthodoxy, Home Rule enabled Gladstone to effect a salutary purge (Cooke and Vincent, 1974, chs 2–6).

Home Rule, indeed, was a well-chosen cause to rally the Radical ranks, as sentiment in its favour, stronger among the electorate than among parliamentarians, was strongest of all among the activists, the crucial constituency workers. Chamberlain left the party, but the great majority of Radical MPs remained, as did the local Liberal associations and the NLF, a major triumph for Gladstone. Strengthened by new affiliations, the NLF was promptly absorbed into central party machinery: its headquarters were transferred to London, next door to the Liberal Central Association, sharing the services of Francis Schnadhorst as secretary, an arrangement which precluded further rivalry (Griffiths, 1976).

Home Rule, then, served to keep the Liberal party Gladstonian, although there were hopes that the new unity, secured at the cost of the (inevitable) secession of the Whigs, would precipitate a more radical and constructive approach. The intellectual establishment, discomfited by Home Rule, turned towards Conservatism, but in some colleges at least Liberal Idealism came into its own, a fitting tribute to T. H. Green. Before his premature death in 1882, Green had redefined Liberal theory, articulating a doctrine of citizenship which posited a positive role for the state, no longer incompatible with liberty. Second-generation Idealists carried the process further. D. G. Ritchie's *Principles of State Intervention* (1891) pointed the way to a collectivist radicalism in which the state created the conditions which allowed individuals to realize their potential. The new philosophy, however, failed to influence the Grand Old Man, guardian of individualist orthodoxy. Having remoralized the party over Home Rule, his last years of leadership were by no means the the seed-bed of Edwardian 'new Liberalism': they witnessed instead 'the death-throes of an individualist politics based on the language of mission and prophecy' (Bentley, 1987, p. 137). 'Irish obstruction' was his constant rhetorical device, a convenient excuse and promise: 'Ireland blocks the way' explained past failings while hinting at reform to come, once the all-important mission had been accomplished. But there was growing impatience with this obsession with Ireland, a feeling much strengthered after the Parnell divorce scandal. In 1891 advocates of programme politics gained the upper hand, prompting Gladstone to endorse the omnibus resolution passed at the NLF's annual conference, the famous Newcastle Programme. A catch-all of various proposals, traditional, faddist and 'new Liberal', this programme embodied four fundamental principles to which all Liberals subscribed to a greater or lesser degree: the extension of political and religious liberties; community self-government; the eradication of privilege and vested interests which conflicted with wider community interest; and social reform to improve the condition of the working class (Bernstein, 1986, p. 10).

Popular with constituency workers, the programme helped the Liberals back into power in 1892. Home Rule, however, remained Gladstone's sole concern − in endorsing the programme, he simply disregarded other items on the list. Having passed the Commons, Home Rule stood no chance of success in the Lords, where Salisbury deployed the 'veto' to telling effect, blocking those measures and 'fads' which lacked an overwhelming popular mandate. Ailing but still obsessed, Gladstone wished to challenge the upper house at the polls following the Bill's rejection, but he was unable to persuade his colleagues. It was now apparent to them that it was not Ireland or the Lords which blocked the way, but the Grand Old Man himself. His final retirement, however − over the cost of naval rearmament — was not the occasion for a new departure. Without his commanding presence the governing party was soon to collapse in disarray.

ROSEBERY

Although identified with social reform and benevolent imperialism, Rosebery, the new premier, was soon to disappoint radical expectations: an old man in a hurry, it was said, had been replaced by a young man apparently in no hurry at all. Harcourt, 20 years his senior, enjoyed greater success at the Exchequer where he acquired a belated reputation for radicalism, the previous absence of which had prevented his succession to the premiership. In his celebrated budget of 1894, a symbolic break with Gladstonian tenets, he envisaged 'a future of ever-increasing expenditure — demands not only for the Army and Navy but for every kind of social reform' (quoted in Brooks, 1986, p. 16). The extra revenue was to be raised in true radical fashion, from landed wealth and drink; privilege was to be curbed by death duties based on the progressive principles of consolidation, equalization and graduation; and temperance was to be encouraged through increased levies on alcohol. At a more pragmatic and partisan level, Harcourt hoped to curb the spread of 'villa Toryism' by raising the threshold for the lower range of income-tax payers, 'the class just above the working class, and which was just beginning to wear a black coat' (quoted in Brooks, 1986, p. 16). Already strained, his relationship with Rosebery deteriorated drastically after the success of the budget. In a bid to capture the initiative, Rosebery mounted a campaign against the House of Lords, an ill-considered exercise which not only exposed further internal divisions but also diverted his attention away from social reform and labour policy at a time of trade depression and industrial discontent, curtailing his efforts to avert 'the cleavage of the classes' by conciliation and reform (Powell, 1983).

Unable to come to terms with personal antagonisms, adverse economic circumstances and the escalating costs of military

42

technology, the Liberals were relieved to forfeit office following their careless defeat on the cordite vote in 1895, when they lost the customary vote of a reduction of the minister's salary by £100 on the army estimates. At the election, Rosebery, Harcourt and Morley each hinted at different programmes — Lords' reform, local option and Home Rule — but none displayed consistency or ardour: the party, indeed, campaigned without any clear policy other than a lacklustre defence of their recent record. Demoralized and divided, the Liberals left 129 English seats uncontested in 1895 — by contrast, the figure for 1892 had been just 23. Unionists took the opportunity to consolidate their middle-class vote and extend their populist appeal, castigating the radicalism of the Liberals which undermined business confidence and infringed the liberty and rights of the freeborn Englishman. Proud champions of the underdog, they protested against the competing Liberal proposals: the licensing restrictions of local option which would deny the poor man his beer in the pub, while allowing the well-off to enjoy the privilege in hotels and restaurants; the inequity of Welsh disestablishment which threatened the endowments of the poor; and the dangers of reform of the Lords which would remove its 'democratic' veto, the constitutional safeguard — 'the heritage of the people for the people' — against 'the chance action of a stray majority' (Brooks, 1986, p. 107).

Recrimination and involution followed the Liberal débâcle of 1895. Social radicals, however, responded in more positive fashion, hoping to transform the party along lines discussed in the new Rainbow Circle. Through the *Progressive Review*, founded in 1896, they advocated 'new Liberalism', economic and social reform posited on 'an enlarged and enlightened concept of the functions of the State' (quoted in Emy, 1973, p. 106). Inspired by Hobson and Hobhouse, distributive justice was the new Idealist aspiration, an ethical and efficient political economy which would reward the industrious while securing minimum standards for all. Financed through graduated taxation of rent and unearned income, social reform was no longer to be considered a cost or burden on the productive economy: by redistributing purchasing power, it would eliminate the

underconsumption of the masses, reducing waste and inefficiency throughout the economy (Clarke, 1978, ch. 2). The need
for a national minimum reflected a variety of end-of-century
concerns. There was a new awareness of the problem of
poverty, a 'consciousness of guilt' raised by social science and
social service, by the shocking revelations of urban surveys and
post-Oxbridge experience in the settlement movement. Concern
about 'national efficiency' spread across the political spectrum
as the economy reached its climacteric, soon to be outpaced by
the productivity and welfare levels of industrial latecomers.
The quest for 'national efficiency' led some social radicals to
support imperialism during the Boer War, abandoning links
with the progressive intellingentsia and the traditional radicals,
for whom anti-jingoism remained the crucial political dividing-
line (Clarke, 1974, p. 165). Campbell-Bannerman, the orthodox
party leader, tried hard to preserve some Liberal unity.

Emboldened to stand forward during the war, Rosebery and
the Liberal imperialists demanded a 'clean slate', an end
to Home Rule and Newcastle-programme faddism, policies
which had cost the party the moderate middle-class vote and
its national self-esteem. These limited intentions notwithstanding, the rhetoric of 'national efficiency' inspired hopes of
major social reform and a wider political alignment. Fabians,
disaffected Liberal Unionists, social radicals and others, left
and right, looked to Rosebery to break the mould, to implement
a new political structure untrammelled by old preoccupations.
True to form, Rosebery was unable to sustain the initiative or
satisfy the radicals, but a more serious hindrance was the lack
of proper organization either at Westminster or out in the
constituencies. Once circumstances allowed, Asquith and other
'Limps' were quick to work their way back to the party main-
stream, leading the Liberal crusade against tariff reform.

EDWARDIAN LIBERALISM

It was this old-style revivalism, not any progressive revisionism,
which brought the Liberal party back into power. Social reform

was an unnecessary extra in 1906, when the Liberals maximized their vote simply by being the 'Not-Conservative' party (Bentley, 1987, p. 110). Outrage over 'Chinese slavery' — the exploitation of indentured Chinese coolies imported into South Africa — fuelled the reaction against costly and incompetent imperial adventures. Anger at the Education Act politicized the Nonconformist conscience, but it was tariff reform which aroused the greatest passion, uniting Liberals of every description. For once, the Liberals were able to mobilize their full voting-strength, boosted by the whole-hearted cooperation of constituency activists, Nonconformist militants, Irish nationalists and Labour allies. The Liberals secured 401 seats, a landslide victory over a party which appeared hesitant and divided, a detrimental image magnified by Balfour's unconvincing middle-of-the-road pronouncements on fiscal policy (Russell, 1973).

Having gained power by revivalism, the Liberals looked to progressivism to add an attractive gloss to their remarkable victory, to consolidate support particularly among the working class. While constituency activists and traditional supporters awaited legislation on education, temperance and Ireland, social radicals were encouraged to project a new party image. According to the new orthodoxy among historians, they effected a virtual regeneration, the long-awaited adjustment to class politics which enabled the Edwardian Liberal party to flourish through its socio-economic appeal to working-class voters. By seizing the ideological initiative, they were able to contain and subsume independent Labour, the socialist spectre which haunted 'organicist' intellectuals (Pugh, 1982, chs 6—7). However, there were ironies and contradictions in this progressive project, serious flaws ignored by some historians. In adjusting to working-class politics, Liberals still denied the very validity of class: progressive Liberals hoped to prevent class polarization, to eradicate the contentious issue of class itself. No longer guaranteed by *laissez-faire* individualism, social harmony was to be underwritten by limited collectivism, intervention sufficient to ensure distributive justice for the working class while preserving free trade and the continuance of capitalism.

45

No mere intellectual fashion, progressivism established a prominent position in Edwardian political debate. An array of talented newspaper editors spread the message, including C. P. Scott of the *Manchester Guardian*, H. W. Massingham of the *Nation*, and A. G. Gardiner of the *Daily News*, the cheap radical paper widely read by provincial activists. The changing social composition of the ranks of Liberal MPs strengthened the progressive element: each intake included increasing numbers of the professional middle class, often educated and trained in the Balliol-Whitechapel ethic of social responsibility. Although the Liberal business connection was weakening, there was no shortage of funds from 'progressive' industrialists who appreciated the value of conciliation, collectivism and distributive justice, causes supported by Lever, Brunner and the Cadbury and Rowntree families (Pugh, 1982, pp. 117—18). But other industrialists displayed no such interest. Representatives of the great staple industries, they responded to increased competitive pressure by retreating further into old-fashioned orthodoxy, rejecting protectionism and progressivism alike — 'the traditional Liberal industrialist in the West Riding of Yorkshire or the Lancashire mills, stiff with pound notes, chapel principles and free trade, still existed on the Liberal benches in 1914' (Bentley, 1987, p. 29).

Progressivism, then, did not carry all before it. Out in the constituencies, most activists still concerned themselves with the unfinished business of the Newcastle Programme. On the parliamentary benches and in Campbell-Bannerman's cabinet, orthodoxy and retrenchment dominated the proceedings. After Asquith's succession, Churchill and Lloyd George, lone apostles of the new Liberalism, enjoyed greater influence and power, but the new premier, a pragmatic imperialist, recoiled from any philosophcal commitment, progressive or otherwise. Judging by the archives of those at the top, progressivism was not the adminstration's motivating force, merely an occasional rhetorical gesture.

Progressivism added an attractive gloss and specious unity to the various 'welfare' reforms introduced by the Liberals. Prompted and determined by different demographic, institutional and political factors, the reforms were 'designed to make the minimum possible alterations in the working of the British economy, to ensure its survival at a time when it was subject to internal and external pressure' (Hay, 1975, p. 13). In matters of finance, however, the reforms were distinctly new Liberal, sharply distinguished from the protectionist prescriptions of Unionist social reformers, shocked into collectivist social reform by the Boer War revelations of physical deterioration. In part prefigured by Harcourt, the new Liberal fiscal policy was elaborated by Asquith in his budget of 1907, which asserted the principle of income differentiation: all unearned income was to be taxed at the new higher rate of 1s (5p) in the £. Despite Asquith's recognition of the need to plan ahead for rising expenditure on social reform, the cost of the Liberals' non-contributory old-age-pension scheme added considerably to the deficit which Lloyd George had to address in 1909. In drawing up his famous budget, he did not envisage its rejection by the upper house: rather, he hoped to use the privilege of a money bill to gain legislative entry for measures recently rebuffed by the Lords' veto of unrepresentative 'fads'. But when the Lords acted in defiance of history and constitutional precedent, he exploited the controversy to the full. Progressivism finally acquired tangible and popular form as Lloyd George's 'People's Budget'.

The constitutional crisis enabled Lloyd George to unify and mobilize the industrious classes, those who worked for a living, against the parasitic landowning class, rentiers who refused to contribute to national needs. In this populist form, progressivism served to legitimize the leadership of the Liberal middle class, industrious and responsible citizens of wealth who recognized their obligations, fiscal and otherwise, to improve the nation's welfare and maintain its defences. A triumph of rhetoric, Lloyd George's tactics kept the Labour party loyal and subordinate. Junior partners in the 'progressive alliance', they reduced their candidates from 78 to 56 between the January and December elections to assist the Liberal cause. As applied in 1910, the electoral pact between the parties helped to curb Unionist recovery, to prevent their regaining working-class seats in London (P. Thompson, 1967, pp. 169–75), Lancashire and other former strongholds lost in 1906. The Unionists obtained 46.8 per cent and 46.6 per cent of the votes in the 1910 elections, but with 273 and 272 seats respectively they remained some way short of the majority necessary for the recovery of office.

After the Liberals' three successive electoral victories, contemporary intellectuals and journalists looked forward to a 'progressive' future. Such confidence was justified, some historians maintain: before the war, there was apparently no reason to doubt the long-term viability of the 'progressive alliance'. In origin, this was no more than a secret electoral pact negotiated in 1903 between Herbert Gladstone, Liberal chief whip, and Ramsay MacDonald, secretary of the new Labour Representation Committee (LRC), an agreement not to stand against each other in certain constituencies, in order to deny the Unionists the advantage of a split progressive vote. At first, the arrangements worked to Labour's advantage: possessing no more than wrecking power, the new party gained its parliamentary breakthrough by courtesy of the pact – in 1906, 24 of the 29 LRC MPs won by virtue of Liberal withdrawals. Thereafter, the Liberals secured considerable satisfaction from an alliance which allowed them to contain independent Labour and counteract the Unionist bias in the electoral system. Upon these electoral arrangements some social radicals wished to construct an ideological accommodation, an intellectual synthesis extending beyond traditional boundaries, Liberal and socialist, to embrace the functional force of progressive thought on distributive justice, industrial conciliation and social democracy, while upholding the principles of individual liberty, equality of opportunity and reward for initiative. Intellectually attractive as it may have been, such progressivism failed to address the everyday realities of class at local and constituency level, political practicalities which, as the next chapter will show, were increasingly to impede the electoral pact. As it was, the arrangements held in 1910 because of the exceptional constitutional crisis. It was not new Liberalism which brought out the vote but another revivalist campaign, an old-fashioned crusade against the abuse of power and privilege, the peers versus the people.

Progressivism was region-specific, restricted in influence largely to Lancashire where Liberals retained the former Tory working-class vote on a platform of social reform prescribed by C. P. Scott (Clarke, 1971). Elsewhere, the new formula was seldom in evidence. A bastion of Nonconformity, Welsh Liberalism continued to dominate the principality without any adjustment in programme or personnel, an unreconstructed force which Lloyd George could not ignore — a new Liberal in England, he was an old Liberal in Wales (Morgan, 1974, p. 170). Traditional loyalties still applied in north-east England, where 'old Liberalism' enjoyed a continuing vitality among Nonconformists, industrialists, businessmen and working-class voters (Purdue, 1981, p. 23). In Yorkshire there was a stronger Labour challenge, but the Liberals largely held their own without any significant change in style. Progressivism excited little interest, much to the disappointment of such local proselytes as Walter Runciman, whose electoral victories at Dewsbury 'sprang from the unexhausted seam of nineteenth century Liberalism' (Pugh, 1978a, p. 1155), and the hapless W. P. Byles, a Bradford newspaper proprietor and editor, forced to decamp across the Pennines in search of a readership sympathetic to new Liberalism (Laybourn and Reynolds, 1984, pp. 82−9).

At Westminster, a progressive influence continued to operate, boosted by National Insurance, a major initiative delayed by the constitutional crisis, much to the impatience of Lloyd George. While the Constitutional Conference proceeded, he was also involved in other forms of negotiation: exploratory talks to establish a new political framework, a party coalition to expedite social reform, national efficiency and Home Rule, and hard bargaining with the various vested interests, public, voluntary and commercial, antagonized by his insurance proposals. Coalitionism was abandoned soon after the conference collapsed, when the Liberals, having wasted the best part of a year, returned to the polls, armed with the King's promise, albeit reluctant, to create the necessary peers should the Lords refuse to pass the Parliament Bill. Introduced shortly afterwards, health insurance differed significantly from Lloyd George's original intention: widows' and orphans' pensions were abandoned to conciliate the powerful industrial insurance companies, who were incorporated in the scheme as 'approved societies' along with working-class friendly societies through whom state benefits might be paid. Unpopular at the time, the insurance principle fulfilled new-Liberal requirements and was soon to enter the political consensus: in assuring minimum standards, it encouraged thrift, avoided unacceptable increases in direct taxation or the introduction of tariffs, and provided an automatic test of eligibility. At the Exchequer, Lloyd George continued to extend the graduated thrust of fiscal progressivism, insisting in his 1913 budget that increased expenditure not only on armaments but also on education, grants in aid, old-age pensions, labour exchanges, and health and unemployment insurance was 'not an extravagance but a real economy – an economy of time, strength, nerve and brain . . . It undoubtedly increases the efficiency of the nation' (quoted in Read, 1979, p. 472). But social reform lost priority after 1911 as the Liberals, dependent on Irish support in the Commons, were compelled to attend to Home Rule, Welsh disestablishment and entry into war.

In an effort to rally progressive spirits – and divert attention from his unwise and indiscreet share-dealings in the Marconi scandal – Lloyd George launched his 'Land Campaign' in the autumn of 1913, following a massive 'Land Enquiry'. The principle of minimum standards was to be extended to the countryside where the disastrous weakening of British agriculture had continued unchecked since the late-Victorian depression, causing serious social, economic and strategic problems. An intervention to improve the workings of the market, the campaign was distinctly new-Liberal and in no sense socialist, but a real economic transfer was perforce required to raise the level of agricultural wages. True to the Liberal animosity against landowners, the cost was to fall not on farmers' profits but on rent, already singled out for special taxation by the People's Budget. A 'wildfire' success in the counties (Offer,

1981), where the prospect of a decent wage was irrestistible, the Land Campaign failed to excite interest in the towns, despite Lloyd George's efforts to proffer a solution to urban finance, trapped in the scissors of rising needs and stagnant revenue. Through site-value rating and other prescriptions of the vociferous land-tax lobby, he hoped to stem the ratepayer revolt into Unionism at municipal elections, to relieve the burden on small property-owning ratepayers and small businessmen. But in this urban context it proved far more difficult to isolate and penalize rent. The bulk of urban property was composite in nature. In the absence of a clear-cut division between parasitic owners of the ground and enterprising capitalists, Lloyd George's rhetoric − as Chamberlain's before − served to antagonize urban capitalist proprietors. Confronted by new Liberalism, property allied more firmly with the Unionist cause (Gilbert, 1976; Offer, 1981, ch. 22).

5

Labour and the Progressive Alliance

The Liberals' electoral success in Edwardian Britain can be explained in terms other than progressivism, but this ideological initiative was designed to secure the party's long-term future, to avert a class-based socialist challenge once politics became fully democratic. Ideological adjustment, however, was not the main requirement. Progressive intellectuals doubtless produced an attractive synthesis of liberalism and the 'higher' ethical and humanitarian features of socialism, but they failed to address the practical problems within Lib-Labism, points of tension which were to provoke a working-class desire for political independence. A symbol of pride and independent achievement, the Labour party was to give institutional expression to a working-class consciousness in which ideology, socialist or otherwise, was of little concern.

THE ORIGINS OF LIB-LABISM

The electoral origins of Lib-Labism were inauspicious, the consequence of secret negotiations after the 1867 Reform Act between George Howell, an ex-bricklayer turned professional labour leader, and George Grenfell Glyn, the Liberal chief whip. Using a 'special fund' and the organizational network of the Reform League of which he was secretary, Howell undertook to investigate the voting intentions of the much-enlarged urban electorate, and to promote designated Liberal candidates, thereby preventing independent working-class candidates from splitting the radical vote. Too susceptible to Liberal blandishments, Howell sacrificed the independence of the League without securing any real concessions over policy and working-class representation – a handful of League members, Howell included, were encouraged in their candidacies in hopeless constituencies, but other labour leaders were compelled to withdraw in favour of Whigs and other party nominees. The Reform League was disbanded in post-election recriminations, but Lib-Labism was by no means discredited.

Through the formation of the Labour Representation League, Howell and the leaders of the 'new model' amalgamated trade unions hoped to renegotiate the terms of the pact, to prevail upon the Liberals to accept a small band of working-class MPs in return for electoral support throughout the land. This limited objective was briefly but dramatically revised when Gladstone's first ministry, having granted legal recognition and financial protection to the unions, introduced the Criminal Law Amendment Act, a forceful restatement of anti-strike legislation which made those on the picket line liable to prosecution for intimidation, molestation and obstruction. Labour leaders reacted angrily – even Howell recognized the need for 'a Working Class Party' to secure full union rights (Leventhal, 1971, p. 153) – but neither the Labour Representation League nor the new Parliamentary Committee of the TUC had the necessary resources to initiate an independent labour party. The 'Positivists' offered intellectual support, but their enthusiasm 'wavered between a conception of a third party organized *de novo* in the country and a reconstruction of the Liberal Party on the basis of Chamberlain's programme' (R. Harrison, 1965, pp. 290–320). As the 1874 election approached, the TUC, lacking guidance and funds, refused to provide a national lead. In the absence of a coordinated labour challenge, working-class estrangement cost the Liberals no more than 10 to 15 seats. The two labour candidates elected, Burt at Morpeth and Macdonald at Stafford, were returned without Liberal opposition on orthodox programmes unexceptionable to middle-class radicals. Disraeli's ministry introduced new and satisfactory labour laws, but once the legislation was safely on the statute book, the unions rallied behind the Liberals, supporting Gladstone's moral crusade against the wicked Turk and the 'prestige politics' of Beaconsfieldism. The Lib-Lab tradition was firmly enshrined when Henry Broadhurst replaced the exhausted Howell as secretary of the Parliamentary Committee.

LABOUR'S TURNING-POINT?

Independent labour representation became a political and organizational reality in late-Victorian Britain as union membership, previously the preserve of the craft elite, exploded to incorporate (temporarily at least) semi-skilled and unskilled workers. As articulated by the doctrinaire and sectarian ideologues of the 1880s, socialism contributed little to this great leap forward, shunning all contact with the existing labour movement. But socialism inspired a new generation of activists, local leaders and organizers who sought to radicalize working-class associations and secure independent representation through an all-embracing labour alliance. Practical and pragmatic, their efforts were slowly to undermine the old Lib-Lab allegiance of 'reformist' trade unions.

Henry George, no socialist himself, opened the way for the socialist revival as he toured the country challenging the 'invisible hand' of orthodox political economy in canpaigning for 'single tax' on the incremental value of land. Disillusioned radicals, outraged by Gladstone's Irish and imperial policies, quickly passed beyond land nationalization, once the *ne plus ultra* of radical social democracy, to the full socialist programme, Marx's exposition of which was widely available by the 1880s in English translation. As interpreted by H. M. Hyndman, founder of the Social Democratic Federation (SDF), scientific socialism was a rigidly mechanistic creed, an inflexible materialism which allowed no role for the 'trade

54

union fetish'. A dictatorial determinist, Hyndman, a top-hatted ex-army officer and county cricketer, displayed a predilection for 'adventure, show and advertisement', sham insurrectionary tactics — financed by 'Tory gold' during the 1885 general election — which forced William Morris to leave the SDF and found the Socialist League (SL). Inspired by a vision of a qualitatively different way of life, Morris sought first and foremost to make socialists of the working class, a project not to be compromised by electoral politics, industrial militancy or street violence. But the League, a high-minded exercise in educational-revolutionism, was soon appropriated by anarchists who looked to the bomb, not the revolutionary working class, as the agency of human liberation. The Fabians, no less outraged by Hyndman's antics among the unemployed in 1886–7, abandoned all thoughts of working-class revolution. Having adjusted continental theory to English circumstances, the 'Hampstead Marx Circle', the Fabian think-tank, elaborated a strategy of gradualist socialism, concentrating their efforts on existing institutions, on the rational conversion of politicians and administrators. Committed to such 'permeation', tactics which met with some success in the progressive politics of the new London County Council, the Fabians made no contribution to the development of an independent working-class party (Pierson, 1973, ch. 5).

At grassroots level, however, the official pronouncements of leaders and ideologues were of limited significance: ethical fellowship and socialist unity prevailed over doctrinal exactitude and sectarian prescription. Here socialism was the crucial inspirational force for labour's turning-point, as 'realists' and activists pursued a wide 'labour alliance', extending beyond the various socialist societies to embrace the funds and resources of trade unions and other collective associations, the necessary base for an independent Labour party. At this level, socialism was 'the fulfilment of a Labour dream, the completion of a homogeneous movement — in which the trade unions organised men and women for industry, the co-operative movement organised them for the provision of their daily needs and the Labour Union organised them for democratic political

55

action. Socialism was the expression of working-class need in politics' (Laybourn and Reynolds, 1984, p. 36).

Prominent figures in the socialist societies lent their support to this grassroots movement for independent representation, thereby dissenting from official policy. H. H. Champion looked to the Labour Electoral Committee, established by the TUC in the wake of the Third Reform Act, to secure the return of a group of labour MPs who would represent the working-class cause at Westminster in the same single-minded spirit as the Irish nationalists. Forced to quit the SDF, Champion and his *Labour Elector* supported a number of independent candidates, most notably Keir Hardie at the Mid-Lanark by-election of 1888, the beginning of the 'labour revolt' against Liberal domination of constituency politics. By no means a mere personal protest at Liberal control of the selection process, Hardie's candidature was a test of the Liberal party's willingness to recognize 'Labour', and what it stood for, as a separate political force (Reid, 1971, p. 19). Supported by Champion and by J. L. Mahon's Scottish Land and Labour League, Hardie managed to secure a mere 8.4 per cent of the poll, but sufficient interest was generated to establish a Scottish Labour party (Pelling, 1965, pp. 56–69). South of the border, progress was blocked by vested interests and internecine disputes. The TUC, still under Broadhurst's leadership, remained a bastion of Lib-Labism, opposed to any independent parliamentary initiatives. Caught in the middle of wrangles over religion, finance and socialist ideology, Champion emigrated to Australia, having closed the bankrupt *Labour Elector.*

Despite these dissensions socialists secured a foothold in the new trade unions of the late 1880s, a vantage point from which to promote political independence. Working-class activists, educated in socialist societies, refused to dismiss the trade unions out of hand. Working from within, socialists like Burns and Mann hoped to transform the unions into an inclusive and militant political force, committed to a programme of 'palliatives', worthwhile reforms to reduce unemployment, poverty and labour exploitation. Realists rather than revolutionaries, they offered practical assistance rather than ideological instruction to the new unions of the late 1880s, efforts still dismissed by the SDF leadership as 'a lowering of the flag, a departure from active propaganda, a waste of energy' (Hinton, 1983, p. 52). Above all, they encouraged semi-skilled and unskilled workers to exploit their bargaining strengths, to adopt big structures and militant strategies alien to the craft-based traditions of conventional trade-unionism. This convergence of tactical and ideological considerations extended to legislation and independent labour politics. Unable to enforce craft regulation at the workplace or restrict the labour supply, new unions were compelled to advocate legislation — socialist palliatives like the eight-hour day — to consolidate gains won by militant industrial action in favourable market conditions.

The success of new unionism depended on full employment, police tolerance of vigorous picketing and the absence of concerted employer opposition, factors which were not to persist. Abruptly halted in the early 1890s, new unionism failed to capture control of the labour movement: the old Lib-Lab unions benefited most from the membership explosion, sustaining their growth after the boom collapsed in 1891 (Lovell, 1977, pp. 20–9). But the very weakness of new unionism prompted an important political response in the West Riding, where woollen workers, hit hard by depression and foreign tariffs, were defeated in a series of disputes in which they 'confronted the face — sometimes complacent, sometimes oppressive, sometimes just plain stupid — of established Liberalism' (E. P. Thompson, 1967, p. 311). The Manningham Mills strike, a bitter five-month lock-out during which the local Liberal authorites gave staunch support to the Tory employers, underlined the political lesson. Radicals, trade unionists, members of the Socialist League and other local socialists joined together in the Bradford Labour Union to promote labour representation at Westminster and on the town council 'irrespective of the convenience of any political party' (Pelling, 1965, p. 95). Similar labour unions and clubs, offering education, entertainment and political propaganda, spread

57

throughout the West Riding, joining the new trades councils in demanding independent political action and an end to Lib-Labism.

Impressed by these and similar initiatives elsewhere, John Burgess and Robert Blatchford, talented journalists with a populist appeal, advocated a national federation to link these local independent labour parties of non-sectarian socialists, disaffected radicals and politicized trade unionists. As a further boost, independent candidates polled well at the 1892 general election, not least at Bradford where Ben Tillett came near to victory in a three-cornered contest. John Burns and Havelock Wilson, the seamen's leader, were elected at Battersea and Middlesbrough respectively, but both were to seek an accommodation with the new Liberal government. Cloth-capped and proud of it, Keir Hardie remained defiantly independent, shocking the Commons with his proletarian manners and headgear when he arrived to take his seat, won at West Ham on an anti-unemployment platform of land nationalization, municipal workshops and the statutory eight-hour day. At the TUC later in the year, Hardie chaired a small unofficial meeting which decided to call a national conference to unite the 'Independent Labour Parties in Great Britain'. In January 1893, the foundation conference of the Independent Labour Party (ILP) assembled in Bradford, an appropriate venue.

The composition of the Bradford conference was overwhelmingly provincial, working class and pragmatic. More than one-third of the delegates came from Yorkshire, working-class representatives of local labour unions, profoundly suspicious of the handful of middle-class London socialists, G. B. Shaw included, who had travelled north. The object of the new party, delegates readily agreed, was 'to secure the collective ownership of the means of production, distribution and exchange', but the term socialist was not to appear in the party's title or its manifesto, a programme of reforms little in advance of progressive Liberalism. Here the important practical consideration was not to offend the trade unions, whose support was indispensable if independent labour representation, the desideratum of the ILP, was to be achieved at the earliest opportunity. A short-cut to political effectiveness, this 'labour alliance' was pursued with single-minded instrumentalism as Hardie exerted his influence over the new party. Alternative strategies were squeezed out of consideration, much to the chagrin of Blatchford and the Lancashire socialists, advocates of a United Socialist Party, envisioned as a fusion of groups including the ILP and the SDF belatedly purged of sectarianism (Howell, 1983, pp. 10–11; Pelling, 1965, ch. 6; Pierson, 1973, ch. 9).

Despite its pragmatism, the ILP failed in the first instance to attract the official labour movement or the electorate – all 28 candidates, Hardie included, finished bottom of the poll at the general election of 1895. To make matters worse, the TUC introduced new standing orders which strengthened the bloc-voting big battalions, the old brigade, at the expense of socialist trades councils, radical new unions and independent labour politicians, proponents of the labour alliance. Four years later, however, a majority of unions were converted to the cause: in 1899 the TUC agreed that trade unions, cooperative societies, Fabian societies, the SDF and the ILP should confer together 'with a view of securing united political action' (Pelling, 1965, p. 203). At the conference the following year, Hardie and the ILP steered a skilful course between Lib-Lab attempts to restrict the new organization to limited trade-union matters and the SDF's insistence on a clear socialist objective. The labour alliance was duly given institutional form as the Labour Representation Committee (LRC), subsequently the Labour party.

The changing political attitudes of trade unions in the 1890s reflected the geography of industrial location. Lib-Labism remained strongly entrenched on the coalfields, separate parliamentary constituencies dominated by miners whose interests and needs could not be ignored. Here working-class candidates were encouraged to stand on the Lib-Lab platform, an arrangement which the Miners' Federation of Great Britain (MFGB), adequately represented in Parliament, had no wish to alter. Hence, they kept apart from the LRC, fearing that miners' funds would be purloined to support extraneous candidates. Scattered throughout the length and breadth of the land, railwaymen had no such clout at constituency level, a considerable disadvantage for workers in an industry without adequate safety legislation or union recognition. Along with the surviving new unions, the Amalgamated Society of Railway Servants (ASRS) led the call for independent labour representation, not to promote a socialist millenium but simply to protect the interests of workers ignored by Lib-Labism.

It was provincial short-sightedness, not Liberal party policy, which accounted for the exiguous increase in the number of Lib-Lab MPs in the 1890s. The Liberal leadership at Westminster spoke encouragingly of the need for more working-class representatives, but local political practicalities precluded their selection. Constituency associations chose not to offend rich local notables by asking them to stand aside and then defray the expenses of working-class candidates. Labour leaders were to react increasingly angrily to such exclusion. 'We didn't leave the Liberals', Ramsay MacDonald protested: 'They kicked us out and slammed the door in our faces' (quoted in Pelling, 1965, p. 224). As dissatisfaction spread, socialists came to the fore in political and industrial struggles, hastening organized workers towards independence by force of example. With or without progressive Liberal support, socialist local councillors and elected officials demanded the implementation of permissive legislation on housing, sanitation and unemployment relief, along with the inclusion of 'fair wage' clauses in municipal employees' contracts. This local advance was strongest at West Ham, where Hardie and his Labour colleagues gained control in 1898 to promote certain specific demands, a compulsory eight-hour day, improved housing and public ownership of the tramways.

At the workplace, socialists acquired new influence and respect among craft workers as defiant defenders of workplace autonomy. They assumed the leadership when the employers, having crushed new unionism, returned to the courts to affirm their rights and authority at a time of critical change in the labour process and collective bargaining (Price, 1986, chs 5 and 6; Saville, 1967). Unions, it seemed, could now be sued for tortious acts committed on their behalf, a point expressly denied by previous legislation. The principle was put to the test in a famous case in 1901 when the Taff Vale Railway Company was awarded damages against the ASRS for actions by its members during the strike of the previous summer. Although the judgement virtually destroyed the right to strike, some trade-union leaders were reluctant to press for its reversal, since the ruling addressed the crucial question of internal trade-union authority, the control over militants and troublemakers necessary for the effective operation of the new collective bargaining arrangements (Pelling, 1979, pp. 76−8). Union leaders, however, finally rallied behind the LRC and the campaign to reverse Taff Vale, a change of heart prompted by the strength of rank-and-file protest, the scale of the award and the intransigence of the Tory government. This was the moment of final break-through: union-affiliated membership of the LRC rose from 375,000 in February 1901 to 861,000 in 1903, when it was decided to raise a fund for the payment of Labour MPs − a practical necessity ignored by the Liberals − by means of a compulsory levy on the unions.

THE ELECTORAL PACT

Electoral success was soon to follow, hastened by the Glad-stone−MacDonald pact, an arrangement which worked to Labour's advantage in the critical early years. Liberal politicians, fearful of the new party's potential wrecking power, saw no alternative to an immediate electoral understanding, much as they disapproved of Labour's 'class politics'. 'The real policy of those who were interested in the cause of Labour must always be to have their views represented in the Liberal party', Haldane opined, an argument expanded by Lloyd George:

'. . . it is better that you should have a party which com-
bines every section and every shade of opinion, taken
from all classes of the community, rather than a party
which represents one shade of opinion alone or one class

of the community alone ... Liberals are against anything in the nature of class representation ... it was a mistake for the Labour Party to go in for anything like independent class representation. They will realize that sooner or later.' (Quoted in Powell, 1986, p. 391)

But the workings of the plurality system operated against these ideological prescriptions of social and political harmony, aspirations for a new Liberal coalition above and beyond the sectional independence of Labour. By conceding the formal independence of Labour, the pact hardened the organizational divide between the parties and gave the LRC a valuable bridgehead in the Commons, so perpetuating the division of parties deeply regretted by new Liberals. In philosophical terms, indeed, the pact was better suited to MacDonald's version of progressivism, an organic evolution through Liberalism to socialism: 'Socialism, the stage which follows Liberalism, retains everything that was of permanent value in Liberalism, by virtue of being the hereditary heir of Liberalism' (quoted in Barker, 1974, p. 124). Defined in this way, socialism served to distinguish Labour as the vanguard of progressivism, leaders of a cause which embraced the new Liberals. MacDonald always aimed at replacing the Liberals at some stage, a long-term goal which underpinned his enthusiasm for the pact, the essential means of consolidating Labour's initial precarious advance.

Limited, flexible and secret, the pact proved effective in the three general elections of 1906 and 1910, but it was to be severely strained in by-elections thereafter. By no means universal, the arrangements operated in a hundred or so constituencies, many of which would otherwise have been won by Conservatives. In some other places, local activists, Liberal and Labour, put up candidates against all comers, but this did not detract from the utility of the pact in the key constituencies. The arrangements worked best in the remaining two-member boroughs, as at Newcastle, Leicester and Blackburn where the two parties were able to run a single candidate each against a pair of Unionists. Elsewhere, they tried to pair local constituencies: in Cumberland, for example, Labour gave the Liberals a free run in Cockermouth in 1910 while the latter stood down for Labour in Whitehaven, both seats being gained from the Tories in the process (Pugh, 1989).

Despite the complexities of the pact, historians have detected a clear trend in Labour's electoral fortunes. Boosted by the pact, Labour reached its peak in 1906−7, after which support fell away, although losses were obscured by the addition of all but three of the remaining Lib-Lab MPs when the MFGB affiliated to the party in 1909. The elections of 1910 revealed the weakness of the independent Labour vote: in the 35 three-cornered contests in the two elections, Labour candidates came third in 29 cases, second in six and first in none. Worse was to follow in subsequent by-elections. The deaths of three miners' MPs, former Lib-Labs, led to unseemly squabbles over the right of succession, three-cornered contests which left Labour bottom of the poll. All told, Labour contested 14 by-elections between 1910 and 1914, losing four seats and never finishing higher than third. On the eve of the First World War, Labour did not appear an irresistible electoral force (Douglas, 1974). But had the Liberals succeeded in containing Labour? Evidence from municipal politics suggests otherwise, highlighting the points of 'class' tension which were to deny long-term viability to the progressive alliance.

MUNICIPAL POLITICS

By no means uniform across the country, Labour's steadily increasing electoral support in the municipalities was negligible or non-existent in the smaller boroughs, old market-towns and cathedral cities (Cahill, 1985; Cook, 1976; for a contrasting view, see Sheppard and Halstead, 1979). The total local Labour vote rose from 170,000 in 1906 to 233,000 in 1913, but even in industrial areas the party had yet to secure more than a foothold on most councils − 8 of 120 seats in Birmingham, 7 of 51 in Halifax, 2 of 64 in Sheffield, 5 of 36 in Northampton (Bernstein, 1986, p. 14). Bradford was the party's 'municipal beacon', but having gained 43 per cent of the poll at the 1913 elections Labour remained the smallest party on the council, forced into straight contests for seats by an anti-Labour electoral pact between Liberals and Conservatives. This 'anti-socialist' alliance, one of 12 already in operation by 1913, caused little embarrassment to Bradford Liberals, as yet untouched by progressivism. Staunchly individualist, they preferred self-help and charity to municipal provision, relying on 'guilds of help' to relieve unemployment and distress. In standing forward with a collectivist alternative, a social policy better suited to the exigencies of working-class life, Labour attracted increasing support. As the Labour vote rose, Bradford became a centre of the municipal school-feeding movement, in proud defiance of the Liberals' rearguard opposition to such 'municipalisation of poverty' (Laybourn and Reynolds, 1984, pp. 168–9). There was a similar advance at Leeds where the Liberals, no less oblivious of progressivism, depended on the aldermen to retain their position as second party on the city council, Labour having gained 14 elected councillors by the 1913 elections, the Liberals 12 (Bernstein, 1983, pp. 624–9).

Labour's success in the West Riding was secured in the absence of new Liberalism, but there was a similar advance elsewhere as municipal politics belied the rhetoric of progressivism, exposing the limitations of Liberal social policy. Pending reform in local government finance, Liberals remained committed to economy and retrenchment, old watchwords not to be infringed by new policies. In competition with the Conservatives for the allegiance of rate-burdened lower-middle-class electors, they shunned proposals which would raise the rates or interfere with the local labour market. Labour alone defied the tenets of orthodox municipal finance, promoting a programme which reflected the needs and demands of ILP socialists and other activists, members of the affiliated bodies responsible for constituency organization: the faddists, as it were, in the party's federal structure. In Scotland, where there was no electoral alliance, socialists concentrated their energies on municipal politics. 'The purpose of Socialism', the Glasgow ILP averred, 'is to capture our municipal institutions in order that they may be used as a means of practically advancing the Socialistic programme in politics' (*Forward*, 13 October 1906, quoted in Smith, 1984, p. 36). As well as campaigning to extend 'municipal socialism' beyond natural monopolies to the provision of milk, coal, health care and other services, Labour activists in England insisted on the right to work or relief, a basic demand which their Liberal allies failed to acknowledge (Bernstein, 1983, p. 638). Dissatisfied and disillusioned, Labour was to abandon the alliance in many towns, but such independence tended, of course, to benefit the Conservatives. As the radical vote split, the Tories consolidated their control of municipal councils in most of the larger cities, including London, Birmingham, Manchester and Liverpool. At this stage, hard-pressed Liberals − particularly in predominantly working-class boroughs like West Ham, Poplar and East Ham − sought an accommodation with the Conservatives, a municipal alliance in negation of their progressive pretensions.

Leicester, the 'quintessential heartland of the Lib-Lab pact' (Lancaster, 1987), was no exception to this sequence of events. Intended as a model, the Leicester electoral arrangements extended beyond the two-member parliamentary constituency, shared by Broadhurst and MacDonald, to cover local elections. In 1903, progressive alliance candidates romped home, gaining almost 70 per cent of the votes cast, but four months later, Labour was compelled to abandon the pact to field independent candidates in elections for the Board of Guardians. In the interim, Leicester had begun to experience structural un-employment and considerable distress as adult males, the main breadwinners of the working-class family, were displaced from traditional skilled tasks in the footwear industry by machinery operated by youths and women. Overwhelmed by applicants, the Guardians at the test-yard persisted with stonebreaking, oakumpicking and woodchopping, ill-remunerated and degrad-ing tasks which offended the dignity of the once-proud artisans. Labour protested at their plight, insisting on decent municipal work at proper wages, demands rejected by the Liberals on grounds of economy. A matter of degree and cost, this issue rapidly eradicated the previous alliance goodwill. As the parties polarized, the middle-ground of working-class Lib-Labism disappeared. By 1906, the Liberal party machine had virtually collapsed in most working-class areas. Removed from office by this division in the progressive vote, Leicester Liberals were obliged to acknowledge a three-party system in which Labour was completely independent of their influence. Having entered a tacit alliance with the Conservatives, they were still unable to contain Labour's advance towards parity: after 1913, the elected representatives on the town council were 18 Liberals, 16 Conservatives and 14 Labour; on the Board of Guardians, the results were even closer, with 16 Liberals, and 15 each for the Conservatives and Labour (Bernstein, 1983, pp. 629—37; Lancaster, 1987, ch. 11).

Elsewhere Labour was less well-placed to mount an independent challenge. Even so, the rejection of the Liberal alliance still occurred, as at Norwich, where the structure of the workforce, predominantly female, casual, non-unionized and voteless, denied Labour a strong electoral influence (Bernstein, 1983, pp. 618—24). Local arrangements continued to operate to mutual advantage in Wigan, Wakefield and Derby, but in most other towns progressive unity was a fiction except during parliamentary elections, special occasions when the lowest common denominator — free trade, the defence of the constitution — temporarily prevailed over the contentious issues of local social policy. After 1910, however, these parliamentary arrangements were increasingly defied by constituency activists. Self-restraint, the necessary precondition for the operation of the pact, disappeared on both sides. Liberal party stalwarts were no longer prepared to make their constituency a sacrificial offering to Labour, while Labour activists, for whom the very purpose of the party was independent working-class representation, refused to stand aside for a Liberal middle-class candidate:

> Labour's desire for continued expansion came up against the Liberal party organization's instincts for self-preservation ... It made little practical difference to Labour whether the Liberal candidate was a Radical or not: it made little practical difference to the Liberals whether the Labour man was a professed Socialist or not. (Petter, 1973, p. 51)

As antagonism intensified, ideological differences mattered less than pride and identity, fundamental 'class' opposition that no alliance could bridge. 'The division', Brougham Villiers noted in 1912, was 'upon the independence of Labour, not upon any economic or political doctrine in any ordinary sense at all' (quoted in Freeden, 1978, p. 149).

The new mood caused considerable difficulties for MacDonald. Although prepared to endorse Labour candidatures in mining seats, he tried to avoid damaging three-cornered contests elsewhere, but he lacked formal authority to enforce the pact, the existence of which remained secret and unofficial. The Labour leadership, indeed, usually denied its existence for fear of offending constituency activists, passionate supporters of independent working-class representation. There was a bitter struggle at Leicester when MacDonald persuaded George Banton, the local Labour leader, to abandon his candidacy when the Liberal seat became vacant in 1913. Treating the election as a vote of confidence in his leadership, Macdonald staked his continued representation of the other Leicester seat on a Liberal victory at the by-election. Much to his relief, the Liberals won by a reduced margin, while E. R. Hartley, candidate of the breakaway British Socialist Party, polled poorly among dissident local activists.

THE PARLIAMENTARY LABOUR PARTY AND LIBERAL REFORM

While municipal politics exposed the limitations of new Liberalism, the progressive alliance continued to function at Westminster much as the Liberals wished, restricting the parliamentary Labour party to a seemingly subservient role. For a brief while after 1906, Labour MPs forced the pace on school meals, workmen's compensation and other social reforms. They were even allowed to dictate the terms of the Trades Disputes Act, restoring full legal immunity to trade unions, the *status quo* before Taff Vale. But this was the last concession to sectionalism as the Liberals seized the initiative with a series of progressive measures which Labour could neither oppose nor amend. Given its precarious parliamentary foothold, Labour could not vote against measures which offered some initial benefit, however inadequate and inimical to working-class interests such reforms might appear to socialist activists. Left-wing discontent was voiced in Ben Tillett's polemic, *Is the Parliamentary Party a Failure?* (1908), an indictment of the careerist toadyism of Labour MPs, repaying 'with gross betrayal the class that willingly supports them'. For activists on the left, unemployment was the test issue. Dismayed by the inadequate response at municipal level, the ILP, SDF and other advocates of 'Socialist Unity' mounted a 'Right to Work' campaign, extra-parliamentary pressure to encourage Labour to adopt an independent, if not socialist, solution to the unemployment problem. Jolted into action by the 1907 by-elections, when Pete Curran beat the Liberals at Jarrow, and Victor Grayson, an independent socialist, contested and won Colne Valley in defiance of party instructions, Labour placed itself at the head of the campaign and drew up a right-to-work bill. This exposed further tensions in the 'Labour alliance', as the TUC was prepared to support the bill, but would have nothing to do with the socialist-led pressure from without. Having failed to pass beyond a second reading in 1907, the bill was to be overshadowed by Liberal initiatives when it was reintroduced in 1909, on the day after Lloyd George presented his budget.

Intended to generate the resources for industrial development and social reform, the budget was an integral component of the progressive social strategy devised by Lloyd George and Churchill. Beginning with labour exchanges, the programme was to extend beyond the budget to invalidity and unemployment insurance. The unexpected constitutional crisis delayed the later stages, but brought the parliamentary Labour party firmly behind the Liberal ranks, tending to conceal differences over the purpose and worth of progressive reform. While restricted to the 'unfit', the pitiful and inefficient poor in the slums, progressive social engineering was welcomed and applauded by Labour (Hinton, 1983, p. 38). When extended beyond the 'residuum', however, Liberal interventionism was far more contentious: while failing to satisfy the socialists, it offended the voluntarist traditions of skilled and respectable organized labour.

Socialists were not ideologically disposed to reject ameliorative measures. As members of the Labour alliance, their priority was the abolition of poverty, not the destruction of capitalism. However, they disparaged reform which fell short of minimum wages and an eight-hour day, the basic demands of the less-skilled unions. Progressivism stopped short of such direct economic intervention, other than for the sweated trades and later the miners, special cases which the Liberals were forced to concede. Here was a basic conflict of approach, a contrast of class interests noted by Tawney in 1912:

> The middle and upper class view in social reform is that it should regulate the worker's *life* in order that he may *work* better. The working class view of economic reform is that it should regulate his *work*, in order that he may have a chance of living. Hence to working people licensing reform, insurance acts, etc. seems beginning at the wrong end. (Quoted in Martin, 1979, pp. 135−6)

In its legislative thrust, indeed, progressivist interventionism converged with employer requirements for greater discipline and control. Labour MPs, however, continued to endorse government intervention, regarding the Liberal state as neutral and beneficent. They supported the new labour exchanges despite widespread fears that a state-run system, as opposed to union schemes already in existence, would serve to supply blackleg labour. Deprived of their control of labour recruitment, male craft workers at Preston were bitterly opposed to new state institutions which enabled employers to undermine the foundations of craft autonomy (Savage, 1987, p. 89).

The 'policing' aspects of National Insurance prompted critical opposition from Hardie, Lansbury and a handful of other parliamentary dissidents. They sought to defend the autonomous structure and traditions of the various collective-self-help agencies through which the working class obtained a range of benefits and services – medical, educational, recreational and welfare – organized and enjoyed in democratic and participatory manner. Some of these associations, most notably the popular friendly societies, were beset with the actuarial problems of an ageing membership: they needed government assistance, not state control. National Insurance was an unhappy compromise: convivial participation and democratic control were sacrificed to the bureaucratic procedures of the commercial insurance industry. Hardie and the critics suspected the Liberals of seeking more far-reaching control over Labour institutions and the working class than was probably the case (Thane, 1985, p. 206), but their concern was surely justified:

> What was at issue was whether the growth of state provision for social welfare would represent an extension of democracy and working-class power, or whether it would tend to suppress existing democratic forms in favour of the construction of a bureauratic welfare machine concerned more with discipline and control than with opening up new opportunities for popular self-government. (Hinton, 1983, p. 76)

In progressive prescription then, social reform was not the formula for success in class politics. Ameliorative welfare legislation was a low priority for most of the working class. They looked to secure 'proper' welfare – cheap bread, decent wages and job security – without state interference. They sought to protect their interests, to 'de-commodify' labour, by free trade, free collective bargaining and voluntarist endeavour. This mutualist mentality was reinforced by continuing suspicion of the state, a legacy of the stigma of the Poor Law and the injustices of the legal system (Pelling, 1979, pp. 1–18). While Labour felt compelled to endorse Liberal reform, the party was sedulous in defence of the legal framework for voluntarist mutuality. Protected by Labour, unions were able to resist repeated attempts to curb the strike weapon and separate their benefit and bargaining functions. A cushion against adversity, the 'friendly' funds were an indispensable part of union strategy for attaining higher wages, the best 'welfare' of all. As well as sickness and sometimes superannuation allowance, benefits included unemployment pay for members refusing to work at below trade-union rates, or made jobless as a result of a dispute in an adjacent trade (Thane, 1985, pp. 185–6). In defending trade-union rights and procedures, Labour thus upheld the essential features of labourist ideology: the labour theory of value was to be implemented by worker's self-reliance, through bargaining and negotiation over the system by which labour power was bought and sold (Foote, 1986, pp. 8–11).

Impressed by Labour's defence of free collective bargaining, the leaders of the refractory unions, miners included, quickly abandoned their former Liberal allegiance. News of the MFGB's conversion, a consequence of worsening industrial relations and adverse legal decisions in the coal industry, caused dismay in some quarters, prompting Shaw to ask: 'What then becomes of socialism?' But this transfer of allegiance, the effective end of Lib-Labism, guaranteed Labour's long-term independence despite its immediate financial problems. The Osborne judgement of 1909 rendered illegal the political levy by which the affiliated unions financed the party. A severe embarrassment, the ruling exacerbated Labour's electoral difficulties: a 'shower of injunctions' fell upon unions which proposed to assist parliamentary candidates (Douglas, 1974, p. 111). Despite considerable pressure, Liberals offered no assistance to their progressive allies – Lloyd George even entered secret negotiations with the Unionists to block a reversal of the Osborne judgement – although they did in 1911 introduce payment of members as a *quid pro quo* for Labour support of National Insurance. The Unionists were no more sympathetic, having failed to generate interest in their own Conservative Labour Unions and the abortive Unionist Labour Party. The ruling was not reversed by the Trade Union Act of 1913, but unions were permitted to hold a secret ballot on the issue. By 1914, ballots had been held in unions with an overall membership of 1,207,841: of more than 420,000 members who voted, 298,702 were in favour of financing Labour candidates, and 125,310 against. While union leaders clearly favoured the Labour alliance, a minority of the membership — nearly 40 per cent of those who voted in ballots in the nine largest unions in 1913 — were opposed to funds being used to support independent Labour (Wrigley, 1985, pp. 133–9, 152). This opposition, by no means an indication of popular support for progressive new Liberalism, reflected the residual loyalty to old Gladstonian Liberalism, most notably among the miners.

INDUSTRIAL UNREST

While Labour was pressing for the reversal of the Osborne judgement, the trade-union movement underwent an explosion of militancy and organization, a much greater leap forward than the new unionism of 1889–90. The 'strike wave' of 1911–13, one of a series in British labour history, represented 'not merely an escalation of overt conflict between workers and employers, but also a shift towards more inclusive organization of less skilled workers, together with an upsurge of rank-and-file activism, a rejection of the cautious advice of established officials, and a renewed emphasis upon the efficacy of strike activity' (Cronin, 1982, pp. 74–5). Total union membership, which stood at 2,513,000 in 1907, rose to 4,145,000 by 1914, while the total working days lost by stoppages, 2,150,000 in 1907, reached no less than 40,890,000 in 1912. Committed to industrial and class harmony, progressivism was unable to contain militancy of this order.

'The era of strikes and lockouts is — or, at any rate ought to be — over,' Lloyd George boldly proclaimed in 1908: 'They really do not settle the justice or injustice of any point in dispute' (quoted in Wrigley, 1976, p. 59). Discord and strife were to be eradicated by trade boards, a corporatist solution in line with legislation of the 1890s, upon which basis Lloyd George intervened in the railwaymen's dispute of 1907. Trade and conciliation boards, however, were never trusted by the unions: they were swept aside as inflationary militancy gathered pace. Taking advantage of the tight labour market from 1910, workers demanded redress for falling real wages and for grievances over hours, conditions and the pace of work, problems which had accumulated at shopfloor level during the preceding industrial truce. Worker unrest took a particularly militant form, fed by resentment at income inequality. As real wages fell, thwarting the workers' rising expectations, the Edwardian leisure class shed all inhibitions, indulging in ostentatious display of conspicuous wealth. Reluctant to abandon conciliation, Lloyd George hoped to restore social and industrial harmony through compulsory state arbitration: 'he saw that if industrial, and hence class, antagonisms could largely be taken out of politics, syndicalism and socialism would be permanently restrained and parliamentary Labour made safe for the Liberal Party' (Middlemas, 1979, p. 66).

Unions tended to resent government intrusion, fearing that the state would inevitably favour the employers, but the dramatic and not unsatisfactory nature of Lloyd George's last-minute interventions in strikes and lock-outs seems to have encouraged some of the stronger unions to eschew compromise within their conventional bargaining arrangements. But there was another side to government intervention: the use of troops and the deployment of gunboats against strikers. This repressive violence and display of force was favoured by some previously noted for their progressive views. Churchill 'was practically in a "shoot' em down" attitude' by the middle of 1912 (Lucy Masterman, quoted in Howkins, 1977, p. 157). C. P. Scott, the *eminence grise* of progressivism, failed to understand the realities of industrial action. Oblivious of the consequences to the working-class Liberal vote in the Lancashire heartland, editorials in the *Manchester Guardian* castigated the 165,000 power-loom weavers locked out in 1911 over their demand for a closed shop: 'The employers are facing an attack of a peculiar kind which even many of those who are firm believers in trade unionism must at present find great difficulty in justifying or even excusing' (quoted in White, 1977, p. 149). Throughout the country, industrial unrest strained the progressive alliance to breaking point, often prompting the decisive switch at local level from Liberalism to an independent working-class position. Fearful of antagonizing their middle-class and gentry support, East Anglian Liberals kept distant from the lengthy farmworkers' strike at St Faiths in 1910–11. Formed to consolidate Liberal victories in the region in 1906, the Eastern Counties Agricultural Labourers' and Small Holders' Union duly abandoned Liberal patronage and turned to the ILP for support (Howkins, 1977).

Industrial unrest challenged the traditional sociological and ideological horizons of the labour movement. From its focus in the most rapidly expanding sectors, coal-mining and transport, militancy spread across the economy. Often unofficial in origin, strike action brought previously unorganized workers flocking into unions: general unions catering for the less-skilled grew fastest of all, finally fulfilling the promise of new unionism. Socialists and syndicalists stood forward to advocate direct industrial action in preference to the parliamentary methods and lacklustre performance of the Labour party. Reforms were to be wrested from the capitalist state through concerted industrial force, following the example of the miners, who brought the whole economy to a halt through national strike action until Lloyd George intervened in 1912 to concede some of their key demands, including minumum wages.

In the first flush of industrial enthusiasm, the British Socialist Party (BSP) came into being, an alliance of the SDF (known since 1907 as the Social-Democratic Party), Clarion groups, 40 or so defecting branches of the ILP, and other unattached local socialist groups. Its initial success owed much to the popular appeal of Victor Grayson, to a personal flamboyance which displeased the 'ethical socialists' of Colne Valley where he was unseated by the Liberals in 1910 (Clark, 1981, ch. 11). Grayson, however, was soon to withdraw, in part out of ill-health, but mainly in anger at Hyndman's ruinous behaviour. Having gained control of the new party, Hyndman and the 'old guard' of the SDF enforced old-style sectarianism, refusing to interfere with the industrial responsibility of trade unions. This self-defeating stance, 'a prime example of the triumph of dogma over realism in socialist politics' (Hinton, 1983, p. 94), prevented the BSP's further development. Membership declined by nearly two-thirds between 1912 and the outbreak of

74

war. Similarly, the ILP failed to effect a socialist advance. Individual members participated in the strikes, but the leadership, still committed to the 'Labour alliance', strongly disapproved of unofficial militancy.

Where organized socialism disappointed, syndicalism inspired, particularly as practised by Tom Mann, eclectic thinker and ceaseless agitator. By no means responsible for the strike wave, Mann and the syndicalists stood forward to prolong and widen disputes, encouraging rank-and-file self-activity, solidarity across craft and sectional barriers, and sympathetic strike action. While weakening the 'class enemy', industrial militancy would heighten workers' consciousness in preparation for the final and decisive general strike. In seeking workers' control through industrial action, syndicalists appeared to reject parliamentary methods out of hand. 'There never was, and there never will be "independence" in parliamentary politics,' *The Syndicalist* insisted in September 1912: 'Even with a separate Labour Party, compromise reigns supreme; there are conferences, committees, bargainings, and what not, with the political parties of our employers ... *Down* with parliamentary politics that divide the workers, and *Up* with Direct Action that unites them' (quoted in Wrigley, 1985, p. 150). In practice, however, syndicalism shaded over into a militant parliamentarianism which stressed the necessity of coordinating industrial and political tactics, a point conceded by the authors of *The Miners' Next Step* (1912).

Syndicalism attained considerable influence among South Wales miners and sections of the railwaymen and dockers, but there was no further advance. There were internal divisions over how to progress beyond the strikes, how to transform the unions first into the agents of class war and then into the administrative framework of the socialist commonwealth. The Socialist Labour Party, a breakaway group from the SDF, advocated the construction of new revolutionary unions outside of and opposed to existing structures. Appropriate elsewhere, such 'dual' unionism was a non-starter in Britain where union penetration was already high, with general unions willing and able to recruit previously unorganized workers. The majority of syndicalists, Mann included, concentrated on education and propaganda within existing unions, narrow and sectional as they were, hoping to canalize rank-and-file militancy into movements for their amalgamation on industrial lines – there was as yet no conception of independent workplace organization as a third alternative (Holton, 1976, p. 205). Syndicalist influence hastened the formation of the National Union of Railwaymen in 1912, which brought all but one of the existing manual workers' unions – the engine-drivers and firemen – into a single industrial union. Syndicalists also assisted the progress of negotiations during 1913–14 for a 'Triple Alliance' of miners, railway workers and transport workers, all of whom had recently been involved in large-scale strikes. As it emerged, however, the Alliance was designed to lessen industrial conflict, not to promote a revolutionary general strike. Union leaders wished to minimize the costs and maximize the strength of their collective bargaining, to prevent further financial loss from unilateral action – the national coal strike of 1912 cost the major railwaymen's union £94,000 in compensation to laid-off members – while increasing the pressure on employers. Confronted by the threat of a combined stoppage, employers would surely be prompted to settle to the satisfaction of unions in each industry. In this way, syndicalism was subsumed as a tactical ploy within the voluntarist framework of collective bargaining (Lovell, 1977, pp. 46–9). Syndicalism, indeed, failed to re-orientate the unions or replace Labour. When put to the vote in 1912, the TUC reaffirmed its commitment to parliamentary action and the Labour party by 1,123,000 votes to 573,000.

Labour marched forward in the pre-war years as trade-unionism expanded. No longer the preserve of the labour aristocracy, national trade unions eradicated regional and traditional loyalties, promoting a wider working-class identity. Some Lib-Lab sympathies still remained, as the ballots on the political levy evinced, but the decision to support Labour, once confirmed in this way, was not to be reversed. In Wales and other bastions, Lib-Labism was in retreat, overwhelmed by the explosion in union membership, the scale of industrial disputes and the emergence of a younger, more militant leadership

(Stead, 1985). Some older miners had still to transfer allegiance, but their leaders were now unquestioning in commitment to Labour: the executive of the MFGB was controlled by Labour supporters as were the executives of all the major district unions (Gregory, 1968, p. 178). In the newly-unionized industries where there was no Lib-Lab inheritance, support for Labour was a corollary of union membership, a point of pride and loyalty which quickly acquired the force of tradition.

Labour, however, was still held back by the franchise factor. For young, mobile and less-skilled workers, the franchise was a more exclusive and restrictive qualification than union membership. In preparation for their eventual enfranchisement, Henderson and MacDonald adopted a long-term strategy. Recognizing the futility of by-election contests, they continued to adhere to the electoral pact with the Liberals, while working towards an independent future by strengthening Labour's organizational structure. Here they avoided any concession to decentralist sentiment. By 1914 local Labour parties had taken over the duties of affiliated trades councils in most large towns and cities, a tribute to Henderson's persuasive powers. MacDonald's successor as party secretary, 'Uncle Arthur' was a frequent and welcome visitor to the constituencies, advising local union and trades-council officials in the complexities of party organization. Where trades councils remained in control, as in the smaller boroughs and county towns, they were encouraged to discharge their political functions more effectively. There was a similar improvement in party finances, a considerable achievement after the setback of the Osborne judgement. Financially solvent, Head Office was able to extend assistance to local parties for election expenses and agents' salaries. By 1914, indeed, nearly all of the reforms associated with the famous 1918 Constitution had been anticipated in some form or other (Leventhal, 1989, ch. 2; McKibbin, 1974, ch. 2).

LABOUR AND THE WORKING CLASS

For those with the vote, Labour offered the working class the chance to return one of their own kind. Although ill at ease in the Commons and unimpressive in debate, Labour MPs were 'closer than their political rivals to the working class; they did not have to try to change their basic character in order to embody proletarian attitudes' (Martin, 1979, p. 142). Lacking in ideological rigour, they personified the values and aspirations of the wider labour movement. Labour possessed the right class image, an asset denied the Liberals, but there were organizational, cultural and other limits to the party's appeal.

Much less exclusive than in mid-Victorian times, collective associations still excluded as bad risks the mass of the urban poor who remained impervious to working-class organization. Before the war, Labour organizers had yet to make contact with the working-class poor, not least in Scotland where local activists 'moved in a rarified atmosphere of the politically militant' (Fraser, 1985, p. 60). Slum-dwellers survived through a life apart, protecting their interests, enjoying their fun in a self-enclosed world of casual labour and neighbourhood support, primary networks into which politics, Labour or otherwise, were generally an unwelcome intrusion (Meacham, 1977).

Indifference to politics spread far beyond the casual poor, as increased leisure-time and rising real wages brought forth rival attractions. Traditional defenders of the poor man's beer and fun, the Tories responded with populist enthusiasm to the commercial mass culture, professional sport and other delights of 'Ally Sloper's Half-Holiday'. Labour was unable to match this style, restrained by the earnest seriousness of leaders trained in chapels and mutual improvement classes. This cultural gap extended to journalism, where Labour struggled to find the formula — as well as the funds — for a national daily: 'The British working classes maddeningly refused to read a Labour newspaper, at least one that did not in more than equal parts report sports and sensations' (McKibbin, 1974, p. 245). Cautious and dull, the short-lived *Daily Citizen* concentrated on electoral politics, the unexciting fare which preoccupied the local Labour press. Ironically, the *Daily Herald*, a modest, unashamedly socialist paper, the product of a rank-and-file strike, enjoyed greater success, assisted by Will Dyson's first-rate cartoons (Hopkin, 1985).

In marked contrast with Germany where the establishment of the Social Democratic Party preceded and controlled the development of industrial, social and cultural associations on socialist lines, Labour in Britain failed to develop its own counter-attraction of a 'movement culture'. Dependent for funds and support on existing institutions, it was unable to establish a comprehensive 'Labour alliance', to subsume the plethora of working-class associations within a counter-cultural party network. The co-operative movement, for example, jealously protected its political independence (McKibbin, 1974, pp. 43—7). Only where trade-unionism and other forms of working-class association were relatively weak, as in Colne Valley, were labour clubs able to propound the 'religion of socialism' (Clark, 1981, pp. 32—6; Yeo, 1977). Labour was first and foremost an electoral machine, in which politics were instrumental in form, not expressive or social. No match for the Primrose League or Conservative working-men's clubs, local Labour parties rarely offered the same corporate and convivial life as the affiliated societies and socialist groups: there were no glee clubs, cycling groups, Sunday schools, orchestras or Cinderella treats.

Hindered or not by the pre-1918 electoral system, Labour was constrained by a number of factors which precluded any advance towards socialism or the unorganized poor: the entrenched power of collective associations, symbols of working-class defensive pride; the rival attractions of commercial popular culture, an apolitical mixture of good-humoured fatalism and brief escapism; and the populist appeal of the Tories, masters of the politics of recreation, entertainment and imperial show. Labour, then, was by no means certain of overwhelming working-class support; hence, no doubt, the lack of pressure for franchise reform. The question of women's suffrage, however, could not be ignored.

This is not to suggest that women had acquired a position of influence within the labour movement. No less clubbable than men, women were concentrated in occupations which were the most difficult to organize: outwork, small workshop and domestic employment, often part-time or seasonal. In 1901 women made up over 30 per cent of the labour force but only 7.5 per cent of the total number of trade-unionists. Significantly, nearly half the total number of women trade-unionists in 1914 were located in the Lancashire cotton mills, where employment was secure, regular and conducted in large workplaces. As well as these structural difficulties, female unionists had to contend against male working-class prejudice. Women's unions still carried the stigma of middle-class philanthropy, instigating force of the Women's Trade Union League (WTUL). Defenders of women's rights, the wealthy patrons of the WTUL disapproved of industrial militancy, but provided the funds to set up unions and undertake extensive parliamentary lobbying, first to oppose protective legislation to exclude women from certain occupations, and then to secure minimum rates and trade boards in the predominantly-female sweated industries. Their efforts were disparaged by the male trade-union establishment. Disdainful critics of middle-class charity, the TUC upheld the principle of the male family wage, sufficient earnings to keep the wife and children out of the labour market. Here, fear of cheap labour and the desire for respectability underpinned an ideology of 'separate spheres'. The ideal of the male breadwinner necessitated the cult of female domesticity, gender roles long enshrined as official labour policy. 'It was their duty as men and husbands', Broadhurst advised the TUC in 1874, 'to use their utmost efforts to bring about a condition of things, where their wives would be in their proper sphere at home, instead of being dragged into competition for livelihood against the great and strong men of the world' (quoted in Liddington and Norris, 1978, p. 37). Despite the expansion of new unionism, old attitudes remained. Speaking in 1914, Will Thorne, the gasworkers' leader, summed up the prevailing male view: 'Women do not make good trade unionists and for this reason we believe that our energies are better used towards the organization of male workers' (quoted in Hinton, 1982, p. 30).

For the WTUL and its offshoot, the National Federation of Women Workers, the priority remained industrial, the struggle to organize and sustain female trade unions, although some of its full-time organizers, talented working-class women like Helen Silcock and Ada Nield Chew, were quick to recognize the importance of the vote. Less hindered by the male trade-union establishment, the Women's Co-operative Guild (WCG) took a more positive line on female suffrage. Founded in 1883, the Guild provided a forum for working-class women to discuss grievances beyond the confines of kitchen and home, training and encouraging them to stand in local elections for school and Poor Law boards, useful political experience to strengthen the claim for the parliamentary franchise. By the end of the century, the ground was well prepared for a radical suffragist campaign led by working-class women from the WCG, WTUL, Clarion groups and textile unions. The new Labour party, however, refused to succumb to faddist pressure to elevate women's suffrage above all else. Most Labour members took an 'adultist' line, preferring to wait for a comprehensive measure of electoral reform embracing all men and women, tactics which infuriated the militants, advocates of immediate remedial action for women. Although the cause of much dissension at party conferences, women's suffrage was finally to prove a unifying force, an issue which distinguished Labour from the Liberals.

Increasingly autocratic, militant and socially conservative, the WSPU abandoned its links with the ILP, after which the various working-class groups fell in behind the adultist line. To this end, the WTUL, WCG and the recently-formed Women's Labour League joined together as the People's Suffrage Federation. Labour, however, came under renewed pressure from the militants when the elections of 1910 deprived the Liberals of their overall majority. The Pankhursts insisted that the party should prove its good faith by opposing the government on every issue until the enactment of women's suffrage. Labour, however, continued to support the Liberals, although Asquith's chicanery over the suffrage, and the forcible feeding of imprisoned suffragettes, prompted George Lansbury to resign his seat to seek a mandate for his suffrage views. In a futile gesture, Lansbury contested the Bow and Bromley by-election with no financial and little moral backing from Labour and the

ILP, forfeiting the seat to his Conservative anti-suffragist opponent.

In the meantime, Henderson engaged in successful negotiations with the moderates of the National Union of Women's Suffrage Societies, a sedate middle-class organization – the Lancashire textile workers apart – which had previously followed a non-party and anti-adultist constitutional stance. Having accepted the proposals of an all-party Conciliation Committee for the enfranchisement of women occupiers, a provision which would extend beyond the wealthy middle class, Henderson was no longer prepared to indulge Asquith's dilatory tactics, his diversionary ploy of manhood suffrage. At the party conference in 1912 he carried a resolution warning the Liberal government that 'no bill can be acceptable to the Labour and Socialist movement which does not include women.' This paved the way for the accommodation with the NUWSS. They offered to raise an Election Fighting Fund (EEF) to assist Labour candidates, finance which was particularly welcome after the Osborne judgement. To avoid undue embarrassment, however, Labour hoped to keep the arrangement unacknowledged, a matter for individual candidates, not the party. Here again, the leadership was considerably more cautious than the constituency activists. The logic of the EFF strategy, MacDonald realized, ran counter to the progressive alliance, which he still regarded as essential (B. Harrison, 1989, pp. 156–8). To shift the log-jam, the NUWSS encouraged Labour to squeeze the Liberals where they were most vulnerable, by fomenting revolt among working-class voters. The government lost four seats in the by-elections in which EFF workers participated. Labour made no gains, but polled well, boosted by the organizational prowess of the NUWSS women, experts in registration, an area of notable Labour deficiency. Although intended as a tactical device, a temporary expedient to be abandoned as soon as the desired legislation was on the statute book, the EFF developed into a wider alliance with labour. Disillusioned with the Liberals, radical and progressive women were among the first of the middle-class groups to

82

switch to Labour. The war accelerated the trend, establishing Labour as the true guardian of the radical tradition, the sole heir to the progressive inheritance (Pugh, 1985a).

6

The First World War

The pattern of political development clearly discernible by 1914 was hastened and accentuated by the 'deluge' of war. Other distortions apart, politics displayed an essential continuity. The Conservatives benefited most. Restored to favour through the rhetoric of patriotism, they were soon to recover their former supremacy, assisted by franchise reform, the unfinished business of Edwardian politics. Democratic enfranchisement was an inevitable consequence of mass conscription, but the Tories were still determined to resist reform of the electoral system, the main topic of debate at the Speaker's Conference. In deference to their objections to proportional representation and the alternative vote, proposals which stemmed from the pre-war experience of progressive politics, Lloyd George withdrew all plans for electoral reform. It was a fateful concession. The combination of a democratic franchise and an unreformed electoral system 'proved to be the most significant decision of the war, for it produced a Conservative hegemony in British Government that lasted until 1945' (Pugh, 1978b, p. ix). The Conservatives were certainly well placed to benefit from the Fourth Reform Act. Recently overhauled, their organization was prepared for the uninhibited electioneering of mass politics; the extension of votes to women on pre-war household-suffrage terms was undoubtedly to their advantage; and they gained most from redistribution. Long overdue, the new boundaries took account of continuing population growth in the Conservative suburbs and its relative decline in rural areas, Liberal Scotland and Wales and nationalist Southern Ireland. The settlement, less favourable than it might have been, still brought substantial advantage: the Conservatives would probably have gained 25–30 seats if the general election of December 1910 had been fought in the redistributed constituencies of 1918 (Kinnear, 1981, pp. 70–2). The Conservatives would not always win under the new franchise and unreformed electoral system, but they would rarely do so badly as to allow victory to others.

The fate of the Liberals is more controversial, given the contention that the party was in good health, rejuvenated by successful adaptation to class politics, until mown down by the 'rampant omnibus' of war (Wilson, 1968, p. 20). But this is to overlook the tensions and strains within new Liberalism, weaknesses and faults openly exposed by war. Put to the test, progressivism failed to uphold radical values or to protect working-class interests. No longer the party of *laissez-faire*, the Liberals were untroubled by the interventionist demands of war until faced with compulsory conscription, an issue which challenged such fundamental values as the individual freedom of conscience. The hawks triumphed, an ascendancy which Asquith, the deposed premier, chose not to contest. There was no attempt on his part to rally the radical forces against the illiberality of total war, no revival of Midlothian and pro-Boer traditions. He continued to support the war effort, but refused to join the new government, a policy which perplexed radicals, pacifists and other opposition Liberals. Disgusted by Lloyd George, disappointed in Asquith, Liberal activists withdrew their support and turned to Labour, seemingly the better guardian of the radical-pacifist tradition – Liberal and Labour candidates in 1918 often commented on the number of ex-Liberal constituency activists running Labour campaigns (Pugh, 1982, p. 201). No longer regarded as progressive, the Liberals were perceived as a party of the right, a change of image which cost them dearly (Hart, 1982). Having lost the support of constituency workers, they were unable to sustain any electoral revival in the inter-war years.

Labour emerged from the war considerably strengthened, a united independent force no longer constrained by the progressive alliance. There were internal divisions over the war, more so than among the Liberals, but these did not prevent the party's advance. Labour gained access to the wartime machinery of state while penetrating deeper into working-class communities. Between the pacifist and patriotic wings, the majority of the party reluctantly concluded that the war was justified, upon which basis they participated in government. But Labour was by no means compromised by coalition politics and industrial truce: working-class interests were protected by extra-parliamentary and 'unofficial' means. Particularly important here was the War Emergency Workers' National Committee (WEWNC), an amalgamation of various organizations – pro-war, anti-war, co-operative, trade-union and socialist – brought together under Labour auspices to defend working-class living standards on the home front. While progressive Liberals concerned themselves with military strategy and the war effort, the WEWNC attended to the more immediate problems of prices, housing, rent control and pensions and benefits for soldiers and their families. Angered by the Military Service Act, the WEWNC took a more assertive line after 1916, campaigning for the 'Conscription of Riches' through taxation, sequestration and nationalization. But this did not presage a forward thrust into socialism, an acceptance of Sidney Webb's collectivist prescriptions. Lacking a coherent ideology, 'Conscription to Riches' was an effective slogan, prefiguring the famous 'socialist' Clause Four of the party's postwar constitution: it provided a rallying point around which the adherents of different ideologies and the representatives of different interests were able to assemble (R. Harrison, 1971; Winter, 1974, ch. 7).

The new party constitution – including the commitment in Clause Four to 'secure for the producers by hand or by brain the full fruits of their industry, and the most equitable distribution thereof that may be possible upon the basis of the common ownership of the means of production' – was designed to consolidate this enlarged 'labour alliance' in preparation for the

Fourth Reform Act. After his resignation from the War Cabinet in 1917 — the occasion for *rapprochement* with the anti-war group — Henderson promptly submitted a memorandum to the National Executive Committee calling for 'the re-organisation of the Party with a view to a wider extension of membership, the strengthening and development of local parties in the constituencies, together with the promotion of a larger number of candidates, and the suggestion that a Party programme be adopted' (quoted in Leventhal, 1989, p. 74). For the most part, the new rules were a formalized version of previous constituency practice. Individual membership, an essential component of the new constitution, was a natural evolution, an important point of entry for disillusioned middle-class radicals. Power remained firmly in the hands of the trade unions, whose dominance of the National Executive, and hence of party policy, was specifically underwritten — in this crucial respect, the constitution 'embodied not an ideology but a system by which power in the Labour Party was distributed' (McKibbin, 1974, p. 91). Having 'exploded' in the pre-war years, the rapid expansion of trade unionism continued throughout the war and beyond: from 2,565,000 in 1910, membership grew to 4,145,000 in 1914 and 6,533,000 in 1918, reaching a peak of 8,347,000 in 1920. This vast extension was accompanied by a narrowing of differentials as wartime controls favoured the less skilled workers at the expense of the old craft elite. Under threat at the workplace, craft workers turned to unofficial militancy, direct action and syndicalism, while the general unions, massive bureaucratic structures, consolidated their control of the official movement. This ironic reversal of roles enabled Labour to continue unchanged while expanding beyond its former sociological limitations.

The predominance of the unions led to an increasing centralization of party organization: the regions were overridden, the Communists expelled, while the co-operators were brought into conformity and the Labour Research Department, the advisory committees and the *Daily Herald* forced into line. Clause Four, however, remained untouched. No mere sop to the professional middle class, this vague socialism was the unifying myth around which the party rallied and asserted its independence. The shibboleth which distinguished Labour from the Liberals, Clause Four carried no ideological or prescriptive force: 'Like "Empire" for late nineteenth-century Conservatives, "Socialism" was for Labour a symbol sufficiently vague to be impervious to mere day-to-day policies and events' (Pugh, 1982, p. 216).

Having emancipated itself from the progressive alliance, Labour was quick to consign the Liberals to the third-party trap, assisted by Baldwin's manoeuvres as Conservative leader. As the threat of 'direct action' receded, the Conservatives decided against an extension of the coalition into a permanent anti-socialist front. Lloyd George was jettisoned and the coalition abandoned as Baldwin sought a return to the normality of two-party politics, but with Labour, not the Liberals, as the chief party of opposition. These tactics were to maximize the Conservative vote, clarifying the party's role as defender of the social order. In the new two-party alignment, 'class politics' came into its own, squeezing the Liberals, victims of the first-past-the-post system, into electoral insignificance. Favoured by the electoral system, and supported by a considerable working-class vote of their own, the Conservatives were henceforth difficult to dislodge. Labour's share of the vote increased dramatically, but it failed to advance beyond the peak of 37 per cent achieved in 1929. The party was compelled to look beyond its natural working-class constituency, to seek the support of the radical middle class (Jones, 1983). This marginal group was to exercise disproportionate influence, shaping the political agenda once inter-war 'safety first' policies were discredited and abandoned. The downfall of the Liberals notwithstanding, progressive 'middle opinion' informed the welfare state of post-war Britain, the Butskellite consensus to which Conservatives and Labour subscribed. Class politics eradicated the Liberal party, but not the spirit of new liberalism.

References and Guide to
Further Reading

Bibliographical details of the works mentioned here can be found in the following References, the length of which gives some indication of the overwhelming volume of material available.

By far the most useful introduction to the structure and operation of politics is the indispensable textbook by Martin Pugh (1982). Extending beyond the period meticulously analyzed by Hanham (1978), Pugh incorporates Peter Clarke's main arguments about class politics and the viability of Progressivism, controversial topics which can also be approached through two summary articles by Clarke (1972 and 1974).

A new crop of introductory texts has appeared, covering each of the parties. Coleman (1988) provides a wide-ranging survey of the Conservatives, taking due account of the recent reassessment of Salisbury's achievement. Bentley (1987), in an important but difficult study, focuses on Liberal high politics, seen through a cynical academic lens. Laybourn (1988) is an up to date, workman-like rehearsal of the various controversies in Labour historiography, to be read in conjunction with the important collection of essays edited by K. D. Brown (1985).

Political scientists bring a different methodology to the study of class and party politics, as can clearly be seen in K. D. Wald (1983), a marked advance on earlier psephological surveys by Blewett (1972) and others. The complex electoral geography of the time is graphically demonstrated by the maps and tables in Kinnear (1981) and Pelling (1967).

Class can no longer be studied in isolation from gender. The best introduction to women, politics and the struggle for the vote is Liddington and Norris (1978), after which readers should tackle the critical review of feminist history by Brian Harrison (1989).

Anderson, Perry 1987: The figures of descent. *New Left Review*, 171, 20–77.

Barker, Rodney 1974: Socialism and progressivism in the political thought of Ramsay Macdonald. In A. J. A. Morris (ed.), *Edwardian Radicalism 1900–1914*, London: Routledge & Kegan Paul, 114–30.

Belchem, John 1990: *Industrialization and the Working Class: The English Experience 1750–1900*. Aldershot: Scolar.

Bentley, Michael 1987: *The Climax of Liberal Politics: British Liberalism in Theory and Practice 1868–1918.* London: Arnold.

Bernstein, G. L. 1983: Liberalism and the progressive alliance in the constituencies, 1900–1914: three case studies. *Historical Journal*, 26, 617–40.

Bernstein, G. L. 1986: *Liberalism and Liberal Politics in Edwardian England*. Boston: Allen & Unwin.

Blewett, Neal 1965: The franchise in the United Kingdom 1885–1918. *Past and Present*, 32, 27–56.

Blewett, Neal 1972: *The Peers, The Parties and The People*. London: Macmillan.

Bogdanor, V. 1981: *The People and the Party System: The Referendum and Electoral Reform in British Politics*. Cambridge: Cambridge University Press.

Briggs, Asa and Saville, John (eds) 1967: *Essays in Labour History*. London: Macmillan, paperback edn.

Briggs, Asa and Saville, John (eds) 1971: *Essays in Labour History 1886–1923*. London: Macmillan.

Brooks, David (ed.) 1986: *The Destruction of Lord Rosebery: From the Diary of Sir Edward Hamilton, 1894–1895*. London: Historians' Press.

Brown, K. D. (ed.) 1974: *Essays in Anti-Labour History*. London: Macmillan.

Brown, K. D. (ed.) 1985: *The First Labour Party 1906–1914*. Beckenham: Croom Helm.

Burgess, Keith 1980: *The Challenge of Labour*. London: Croom Helm.

Cahill, M. 1985: Labour in the municipalities. In K. D. Brown (ed.), *The First Labour Party 1906–1914*, 89–104.

Cain, P. J. and Hopkins, A. G. 1987: Gentlemanly capitalism and British expansion overseas, II: new imperialism, 1850–1914. *Economic History Review*, 2nd ser, 40, 1–26.

Chadwick, M. E. J. 1976: The role of redistribution in the making of the Third Reform Act. *Historical Journal*, 19, 665–83.

Clark, David 1981: *Colne Valley: Radicalism to Socialism*. London: Longman.

Clarke, P. F. 1971: *Lancashire and the New Liberalism*. Cambridge: Cambridge University Press.

Clarke, P. F. 1972: Electoral sociology of modern Britain. *History*, 57, 31–55.

Clarke, P. F. 1974: The progressive movement in England. *Transactions of the Royal Historical Society*, 5th series, 24, 159–81.

Clarke, P. F. 1977: Liberals, Labour and franchise. *English Historical Review*, 92, 582–9.

Clarke, P. F. 1978: *Liberals and Social Democrats*. Cambridge: Cambridge University Press.

Clegg, H., Fox, A. and Thompson, A. F. 1964: *A History of British Trade Unions since 1889*. Oxford: Clarendon Press.

Coleman, Bruce 1988: *Conservatism and the Conservative Party in Nineteenth-Century Britain*. London: Arnold.

Colls, R. and Dodd, P. (eds) 1986: *Englishness: Politics and Culture 1880–1920*. Beckenham: Croom Helm.

Cook, Chris 1976: Labour and the downfall of the Liberal party, 1906–14. In A. Sked and C. Cook (eds), *Crisis and Controversy: Essays in Honour of A. J. P. Taylor*, London: Macmillan, 38–65.

Cooke, A. B. and Vincent, J. 1974: *The Governing Passion: Cabinet Government and Party Politics in Britain 1885–86*. Brighton: Harvester.

Cornford, James 1963: The transformation of Conservatism in the late nineteenth century. *Victorian Studies*, 7, 35–66.

Cornford, James 1967: The parliamentary foundations of the Hotel Cecil. In R. Robson (ed.), *Ideas and Institutions of Victorian Britain*, London: Bell, 268–311.

Cox, Gary 1987: *The Efficient Secret: The Cabinet and the Development of Political Parties in Victorian England*. Cambridge: Cambridge University Press.

Cronin, J. E. 1982: Strikes 1870–1914. In Chris Wrigley (ed.), *A History of British Industrial Relations 1875–1914*, 74–98.

Crossick, G. 1977: The emergence of the lower middle class in Britain: a discussion. In G. Crossick (ed.), *The Lower Middle Class in Britain 1870–1914*, London: Croom Helm, 11–60.

Cunningham, Hugh 1986: The Conservative party and patriotism. In R. Colls and P. Dodd (eds), *Englishness: Politics and Culture 1880–1920*, 283–307.

Dangerfield, George 1936: *The Strange Death of Liberal England*. London: Constable.

Daunton, M. J. 1989: 'Gentlemanly capitalism' and British industry 1820–1914. *Past and Present*, 122, 119–58.

Douglas, Roy 1974: Labour in decline 1910–14. In K. D. Brown (ed.), *Essays in Anti-Labour History*, 105–25.

Dunbabin, J. P. D. 1980: British elections in the nineteenth and twentieth centuries, a regional approach. *English Historical Review*, 95, 241–67.

Emy, H. V. 1973: *Liberals, Radicals and Social Politics 1892–1914*. Cambridge: Cambridge University Press.

Foote, G. 1986: *The Labour Party's Political Thought: A History*. London: Croom Helm.

Fraser, Derek 1979: *Urban Politics in Victorian England. The Structure of Politics in Victorian Cities*. London: Macmillan paperback edn.

Fraser, W. H. 1985: The Labour party in Scotland. In K. D. Brown (ed.), *The First Labour Party 1906–1914*, 38–63.

Freeden, M. 1978: *The New Liberalism: An Ideology of Social Reform*. Oxford: Clarendon Press.

Gilbert, B. B. 1976: David Lloyd George: land, the budget and social reform. *American Historical Review*, 81, 1058–66.

Gregory, Roy 1968: *The Miners and British Politics 1906–1914*. Oxford: Oxford University Press.

Griffiths, P. C. 1976: The caucus and the Liberal party in 1886. *History*, 61, 183–97.

Guttsman, W. L. 1963: *The British Political Elite*. London: MacGibbon and Kee.

Hamer, D. A. (ed.) 1971: *The Radical Programme, 1885*. Brighton: Harvester reprint of 1885 edn.

Hamer, D. A. 1972: *Liberal Politics in the Age of Gladstone and Rosebery*. Oxford: Clarendon Press.

Hamer, D. A. 1977: *The Politics of Electoral Pressure: A Study in the History of Victorian Reform Agitations*. Brighton: Harvester.

Hammerton, E. and Cannadine, D. 1981: Conflict and consensus on a ceremonial occasion: the Diamond Jubilee in Cambridge in

1897. *Historical Journal*, 24, 111−46.

Hanham, H. J. 1966: Politics and community life in Victorian and Edwardian Britain. *Folk Life*, 4, 5−14.

Hanham, H. J. 1978: *Elections and Party Management: Politics in the Time of Disraeli and Gladstone.* Hassocks: Harvester, 2nd edn.

Harrison, Brian 1989: Class and gender in modern British labour history. *Past and Present*, 124, 121−58.

Harrison, Royden 1965: *Before the Socialists: Studies in Labour and Politics, 1861−1881.* London: Routledge & Kegan Paul.

Harrison, Royden 1971: The War Emergency Workers' National Committee, 1914−1920. In A. Briggs and J. Saville (eds), *Essays in Labour History 1886−1923*, 211−59.

Hart, M. 1982: The Liberals, the War and the franchise. *English Historical Review*, 97, 820−32.

Hay, J. R. 1975: *The Origins of the Liberal Welfare Reforms 1906−1914.* London: Macmillan.

Hinton, James 1982: The rise of a mass labour movement: growth and limitations. In Chris Wrigley (ed.), *A History of British Industrial Relations 1875−1914*, 20−46.

Hinton, James 1983: *Labour and Socialism: A History of the British Labour Movement 1867−1914.* Brighton: Wheatsheaf.

Hobsbawm, Eric 1984: *Worlds of Labour.* London: Weidenfeld and Nicolson.

Holton, Bob 1976: *British Syndicalism 1900−1914: Myths and Realities.* London: Pluto Press.

Hopkin, Deian 1985: The Labour party press. In K. D. Brown (ed.), *The First Labour Party 1906−1914*, 105−28.

Howarth, Janet 1969: The liberal revival in Northamptonshire, 1880−1895: a case study in late nineteenth century elections. *Historical Journal*, 12, 78−118.

Howell, David 1983: *British Workers and the Independent Labour Party 1888−1906.* Manchester: Manchester University Press.

Howkins, Alun 1977: Edwardian liberalism and industrial unrest: a class view of the decline of Liberalism. *History Workshop Journal*, 4, 143−61.

Jones, G. S. 1983: Why is the Labour party in a mess? In his *Languages of Class: Studies in English Working Class History.* Cambridge: Cambridge University Press, 239−56.

Joyce, Patrick 1982: *Work, Society and Politics: The Culture of the Factory in Later Victorian England.* London: Methuen paperback edn.

Kinnear, Michael 1981: *The British Voter: An Atlas and Survey since 1885*. London: Batsford. 2nd edn.

Lancaster, Bill 1987: *Radicalism, Cooperation and Socialism: Leicester Working-Class Politics 1860–1906*. Leicester: Leicester University Press.

Laybourn, Keith 1988: *The Rise of Labour: The British Labour Party 1890–1979*. London: Arnold.

Laybourn, Keith and Reynolds, Jack 1984: *Liberalism and the Rise of Labour 1890–1918*. London: Croom Helm.

Lee, A. J. 1979: Conservatism, traditionalism and the British working class, 1880–1918. In David Martin and David Rubinstein (eds), *Ideology and the Labour Movement*, London: Croom Helm, 84–102.

Leventhal, F. M. 1971: *Respectable Radical: George Howell and Victorian Working-Class Politics*. London: Weidenfeld and Nicolson.

Leventhal, F. M. 1989: *Arthur Henderson*. Manchester: Manchester University Press.

Liddington, Jill and Norris, Jill 1978: *One Hand Tied Behind Us: The Rise of the Women's Suffrage Movement*. London: Virago.

Lovell, John 1977: *British Trade Unions 1875–1933*. London: Macmillan.

McKenzie, R. and Silver, A. 1968: *Angels in Marble: Working-Class Conservatives in Urban England*. London: Heinemann.

McKibbin, Ross 1974: *The Evolution of the Labour Party 1910–1924*, Oxford: Oxford University Press.

McKibbin, Ross 1984: Why was there no Marxism in Great Britain? *English Historical Review*, 99, 297–331.

Marsh, Peter 1978: *The Discipline of Popular Government: Lord Salisbury's Domestic Statecraft 1881–1902*. Hassocks: Harvester.

Martin, David 1979: 'The instruments of the people?': the parliamentary Labour party in 1906. In David Martin and David Rubinstein (eds), *Ideology and the Labour Movement*, London: Croom Helm, 125–46.

Matthew, H. C. G., McKibbin, R. and Kay, J. A. 1976: The franchise factor in the rise of the Labour party. *English Historical Review*, 91, 723–52.

Meacham, Standish 1977: *A Life Apart: The English Working Class 1890–1914*, London: Thames and Hudson.

Middlemas, Keith 1979: *Politics in Industrial Society: The Experience of the British System since 1911*. London: Deutsch.

Morgan, K. O. 1974: The New Liberalism and the challenge of

Labour: the Welsh experience, 1895–1929. In K. D. Brown (ed.), *Essays in Anti-Labour History*, 159–82

Neale, R. S. 1981: *Class in English History 1680–1850*. Oxford: Basil Blackwell.

Offer, Avner 1981: *Property and Politics 1870–1914: Landownership, Law, Ideology and Urban Development in England*. Cambridge: Cambridge University Press.

O'Gorman, Frank 1986: *British Conservatism: Conservative Thought from Burke to Thatcher*. London: Longman.

Pelling, Henry 1965: *The Origins of the Labour Party*. Oxford: Oxford University Press. 2nd edn.

Pelling, Henry 1967: *Social Geography of British Elections 1885–1910*. London: Macmillan.

Pelling, Henry 1979: *Popular Politics and Society in Late Victorian Britain*. London: Macmillan. 2nd edn.

Petter, Martin 1973: The progressive alliance. *History*, 58, 45–59.

Pierson, Stanley 1973: *Marxism and the Origins of British Socialism: The Struggle for a New Consciousness*. Ithaca: Cornell University Press.

Powell, David 1983: The Liberal ministries and Labour, 1892–1895. *History*, 68, 408–26.

Powell, David 1986: The new Liberalism and the rise of Labour, 1886–1906. *Historical Journal*, 29, 369–93.

Price, Richard 1986: *Labour in British Society*. London: Croom Helm.

Pugh, Martin 1978a: Yorkshire and the new Liberalism? *Journal of Modern History*, 50, 1139–55.

Pugh, Martin 1978b: *Electoral Reform in War and Peace 1906–18*. London: Routledge & Kegan Paul.

Pugh, Martin 1982: *The Making of Modern British Politics 1867–1939*. Oxford: Basil Blackwell.

Pugh, Martin 1985a: Labour and women's suffrage. In K. D. Brown (ed.), *The First Labour Party 1906–1914*, 233–53.

Pugh, Martin 1985b: *The Tories and the People 1880–1935*. Oxford: Basil Blackwell.

Pugh, Martin 1988: *The Evolution of the British Electoral System 1832–1987*. London: Historical Association.

Pugh, Martin 1989: Handshakes to power. *Times Higher Education Supplement*, 21 April.

Purdue, A. W. 1981: The Liberal and Labour parties in north-east politics 1900–14. *International Review of Social History*, 36, 1–24.

Ramsden, John 1978: *The Age of Balfour and Baldwin, 1902–1940*.

London: Longman.

Read, Donald 1979: *England 1868–1914*. London: Longman.

Reid, Fred 1971: Keir Hardie's conversion to socialism. In A. Briggs and J. Saville (eds), *Essays in Labour History 1886–1923*, 17–46.

Ridley, Jane 1987: The Unionist Social Reform Committee, 1911–1914: wets before the deluge. *Historical Journal*, 30, 391–413.

Robbins, Keith 1988: *Nineteenth-Century Britain: England, Scotland and Wales: The Making of a Nation*. Oxford: Oxford University Press.

Russell, A. K. 1973: *Liberal Landslide: The General Election of 1906*. Newton Abbot: David and Charles.

Savage, Michael 1987: *The Dynamics of Working-Class Politics: The Labour Movement in Preston, 1880–1940*. Cambridge: Cambridge University Press.

Saville, John 1967: Trade unions and free labour: the background to the Taff Vale decision. In A. Briggs and J. Saville (eds), *Essays in Labour History*, 317–50.

Searle, G. R. 1979: Critics of Edwardian society: the case of the radical right. In Alan O'Day (ed.), *The Edwardian Age: Conflict and Stability 1900–1914*, London: Macmillan, 79–96.

Sheppard, M. G. and Halstead, J. 1979: Labour's municipal election performance in provincial England and Wales 1901–13. *Bulletin of the Society for the Study of Labour History*, 39, 39–62.

Smith, Joan 1984: Labour tradition in Glasgow and Liverpool. *History Workshop Journal*, 17, 32–56.

Stead, Peter 1985: The Labour party in Wales. In K. D. Brown (ed.), *The First Labour Party 1906–1914*, 64–88.

Sykes, Alan 1979: *Tariff Reform in British Politics, 1903–1913*. Oxford: Clarendon Press.

Tanner, Duncan 1983: The parliamentary electoral system, the 'Fourth' Reform Act and the rise of Labour in England and Wales. *Bulletin of the Institute of Historical Research*, 56, 205–19.

Thane, Pat 1985: The Labour party and state 'welfare'. In K. D. Brown (ed.), *The First Labour Party 1906–1914*, 183–216.

Thompson, E. P. 1967: Homage to Tom Maguire. In A. Briggs and J. Saville (eds), *Essays in Labour History*, 276–316.

Thompson, Paul 1967: *Socialists, Liberals and Labour: The Struggle for London 1885–1914*. London: Routledge & Kegan Paul.

Tillett, Ben 1908: *Is the Parliamentary Party a Failure?* London.

Vincent, John 1967: *Pollbooks: How Victorians Voted*. Cambridge: Cambridge University Press.

Vincent, John 1972: *The Formation of the British Liberal Party 1857–1868*. Harmondsworth: Penguin.

Wald, K. D. 1983: *Crosses on the Ballot: Patterns of British Voter Alignment since 1885*. Princeton: Princeton University Press.

Waller, R. 1987: The decline of class voting in Britain? *Parliamentary History*, 6, 326–9.

White, Joseph 1977: A panegyric on Edwardian progressivism. *Journal of British Studies*, 16, 145–52.

Wiener, M. J. 1985: *English Culture and the Decline of the Industrial Spirit 1850–1980*. Harmondsworth: Penguin.

Wilson, Trevor 1968: *The Downfall of the Liberal Party 1914–1935*. London: Fontana.

Winter, J. M. 1974: *Socialism and the Challenge of War: Ideas and Politics in Britain, 1912–18*. London: Routledge & Kegan Paul.

Wrigley, Chris 1976: *David Lloyd George and the British Labour Movement: Peace and War*. Brighton: Harvester.

Wrigley, Chris (ed.) 1982: *A History of British Industrial Relations 1875–1914*. Brighton: Harvester.

Wrigley, Chris 1985: Labour and the trade unions. In K. D. Brown (ed.), *The First Labour Party 1906–1914*, 129–57.

Yeo, Stephen 1977: A new life: the religion of socialism in Britain 1883–1896. *History Workshop Journal*, 4, 5–56.

Yeo, Stephen 1986: Socialism, the state and some oppositional Englishness. In R. Colls and P. Dodd (eds), *Englishness: Politics and Culture 1880–1920*, 308–69.

Young, Ken 1975: *Local Politics and the Rise of Party: The London Municipal Society and the Conservative Intervention in Local Elections 1894–1963*. Leicester: Leicester University Press.

Index

socialism, 3, 15, 25, 36, 39, 48, 52, 54–9, 60, 62, 64, 69, 74, 79, 86, 87–8

Socialist Labour Party, 75

Socialist League, 55, 57

suffragettes, 81; *see also* women, suffrage

syndicalism, 13, 74–6, 87

Taff Vale, 61, 67

tariff reform, 16, 29–32, 33, 39, 44, 45

Tawney, R. H., 69

Thorne, Will, 80

Tillett, Ben, 58, 68

trade unionism, 28, 53, 54, 56–7, 58, 60–1, 70–7, 79, 80, 87

trades councils, 58, 59, 77

Trades Disputes Act (1906), 67

Trades Union Congress, 53, 56, 58, 59, 76, 80

Unionist Social Reform Committee, 33–4

'villa Toryism', 4, 11, 21, 42

Villiers, B., 67

Wakefield, 66

Wales, 15, 49, 76, 85

disestablishment, 43, 50

War Emergency Workers' National Committee, 86

Webb, Sidney, 86

West Ham, 58, 60, 65

Whigs, 10, 21, 23, 24, 29, 37, 38, 40, 53

Wigan, 66

Williams, J. E., 39

Wilson, J. Havelock, 58

Wolff, Sir Henry Drummond, 20

women

suffrage, 14, 27, 79–83, 84

trade unionism, 79–80

Women's Co-operative Guild, 81

Women's Labour League, 81

Women's Social and Political Union, 14, 81

Women's Trade Union League, 80